It's Okay to Sleep with Him on the First Date

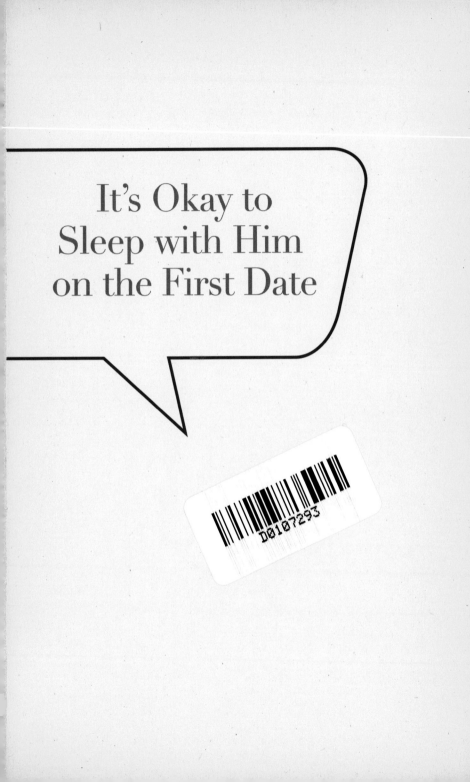

It's Okay to Sleep with Him on the First Date

And Every Other Rule of Dating,
DEBUNKED

ANDREA SYRTASH & JEFF WILSER

It's Okay to Sleep with Him on the First Date

ISBN-13:978-0-373-89278-5

Library of Congress Cataloging-in-Publication Data

Syrtash, Andrea

It's okay to sleep with him on the first date—and every other rule of dating, debunked/Andrea Syrtash and Jeff Wilser.

p. cm.

ISBN 978-0-373-89278-5

1. Dating (Social customs). 2. Mate selection. 3. Single women. 4. Man-woman relationships. I. Wilser, Jeff. II. Title.

HQ801.S983 2013

306.73--dc23

2012041647

www.Harlequin.com

Printed in U.S.A.

To all successful relationships . . . that started
with a hook-up. And to all women who
break the rules every day in order to
live their best lives.
—Andrea

What Andrea said.
—Jeff

CONTENTS

CONTENTS

even dismissed at first glance. (Confession: I'm one of
men.)
ps I don't like dating rules because by their very nature,
imiting. The trouble is, our culture is based on quick
simple solutions. The advertising industry loves to cre-
*ty and aspirational thinking. Their goal is to make you
need that. If I don't get that certain something (or some-
on't be happy.* Unfortunately, the dating industry also
fear-based messages ("You're not getting any younger!")
you into buying into their rules.

n you follow dating rules, you're stepping into some-
's value system. Your friend who insists that you should
sleep with someone on a first date" has every right to
tting too physical early on if that's against her principals,
doesn't mean that this idea reflects yours. If you are
to sex on date one for religious or moral reasons—or just
it doesn't feel right to you—follow your judgment. But
ou want to sleep with him on the first date and you feel
able with that? Nobody can tell you that you shouldn't,
ecause they wouldn't.

're new to dating, it can be very helpful to have clear
ng guidelines and rules. But we trust that you have some
ce in the dating department and at least some under-
; of what works and doesn't work, so we don't want to
ed you these fear tactics. Rules in dating keep you inside
d and out of an experience; they make you question your

INTRODUCTION: ON RULES

It's okay to sleep with him on the first date. It's also okay to not sleep with him on the first date. And it's okay to wait three dates, three weeks, or three years before sleeping with him.

But the old adage "If you hook up on the first date, he'll think you're a slut!" is an adage that's, well, *old.* The world has changed. For better or worse—we think better—our generation is more comfortable with sex, less prudish, and less likely to freak out after a night of boozy fun. Maybe that makes us lushes. We think it also makes us realists.

This rule—like many others—is cliché, outdated, and overly simplistic. Never trust a rule that begins with "Never," and always be suspicious of a rule that begins with "Always." The *Never* rules and *Always* rules are the accepted conventional wisdom, and the conventional wisdom is about a decade behind the curve.

The rules can hurt you.

On the surface, the rules are about your protection, but they have a sneaky way of making us all more insecure, less trusting, less authentic, and less likely to find a match. They breed cynicism. Gimmick-based rules like "Pretend you're busy" can help you in the short-term, but you're less likely to find long-term happiness—and yeah, we'll say it, you're less likely to find Love—by this kind of game playing. Rules like "Men love bitches" make you hide your true self. Or you could miss out on a great catch if you follow the rule "Don't talk to a man first." (Not every guy is good at approaching women, but that doesn't mean he's a lousy boyfriend.) The rules can squash your emotions—*I think I'm loving this guy, but he breaks Rule 34*—they foment doubt, and they make you wear crazy-colored glasses. Dating is supposed to be fun, but how can you be relaxed when you're counting the days between dates and the hours between calls?

You've heard some of these rules before, like "He's just not that into you," "Never date a co-worker," or *The Millionaire Matchmaker*'s "No sex before monogamy." But plenty of the rules are less obvious, more subtle, and they've seeped into the dating ecosystem.

So we'll identify the rules, debate them, and show how they're actually hurting your chances. Written in (rough) chronological order, this book covers the whole spectrum of dating: the overall psychology, the first date, the men you "shouldn't" date, the awkward "this has potential" phase, seeing someone, and then rules about moving in together, engagements, or, less happily, the rules on break-ups. We'll also tackle the rules about social media,

online dating, and the bizarre new etiq
(As far as we know, this hasn't been cov
also included some questions that we

Even though we come from differe
married, Jeff's single—we often reach t
sion. With a mix of research, case studies,
this is a book that cuts through the clutte
We won't promise you a secret tonic to
acronym for Love. This isn't meant to be
can get a date. Our guess is that you go
you. In fact, if there's only one thing we w
book, it's this: *Don't trust the rules, trust y*

So if you want to sleep with him on th
one rule: use a condom.

ANDREA

Over the years, my research, interviews,
men and women have shown one consist
get together: there are no consistent ru
women who preached rules like "Long-
don't work" but ended up marrying some
the country, and women who felt that the
if they wanted to be with a man, only to
madly in love with a person who was not

they h
these
Pe
they'r
fixes
ate a
think
one),
relie
to sc

one
"N
avo
bu
op
be
wh
co
si

a
e
s
s
y

own instincts. And your instincts are better than what anybody else can instruct you to do (or not do).

So why are you reading this book? Shouldn't we stop here if we believe you know best? We may not believe in hard and fast rules, but we do believe in strategies. Strategies are smart. It's helpful to have ideas on how to approach situations or dodge uncomfortable moments in your love life. Tools allow you to widen your perspective, challenge yourself, and think critically, which is always a good thing.

I hope that this book helps open your mind to new possibilities so that you can find more success in the love department (whatever *success* means to you) and that it helps guide you to listen to your best judgment over anybody else's. Choose the strategies and perspectives that resonate, and ditch the rest. My goal is to challenge the black-and-white way of thinking about dating that you've heard for years and to make dating fun again.

While rules tell you *what* to do (and when and why and where to do it), I'd rather focus on the *how*. How can you date more effectively to get closer to your goals? How can you be most authentic in your relationships? How can you quiet everybody else's wants so that you can listen to your own?

Confession time: I'm a rule lover.

Or at least I used to be. The rules helped me flirt, they gave me a jolt of confidence, and they helped me dodge rookie mistakes. I could protect—even hide—my inner geek with rules like, "After you get her number, wait two days before calling." I wore the rules like armor.

Rules imply a world that's governed by order, logic, and reason. They appeal to our sense of gamesmanship. *If we follow the right rules, we'll win.* I liked the rules so much, in fact, that I even wrote a book about them, *The Maxims of Manhood: 100 Rules Every Real Man Must Live By.* Literally an entire book of rules, and not just any kind of rules, but the kind that you *must live by!*

And now, today, I'm saying that the rules are bunk. So how do I square this?

For one thing, the other book was mostly a joke. I don't *really* believe "Maxim 94: Your dog must be larger than a toaster." And some of the rules make plenty of sense—be yourself, don't cheat, use deodorant.

But I have three beefs with dating rules:

1. **They stamp out the nuance of human dynamics,** making everything seem as tidy as Step 1, Step 2, Step 3. Life doesn't work like that.
2. **They spawn relationship "experts"** who claim to have a bulletproof way for you to find love. It reminds me of the world of finance, pre–housing crash: talking heads spewing bad advice, like "Leverage your

mortgage. Buy a bigger home! Borrow more! He's just
not that into you! Wait three days to call him back!"

3. **They don't always work.** As I've gotten older and
seen more of my friends get married—seventeen
weddings since '09—I've noticed one clear pattern:
their happiness has nothing to do with the rules. In
some cases, the woman pursued the man (a definite
Don't); in others, the woman made more money
than the man (gasp!); and yes, some of them hooked
up on the first date. I followed the rules. They
didn't. I'm still single. They're not.

This is the problem with armor: it's great for keeping you safe,
but it does this by hiding your skin, dulling your senses, and
keeping others at bay.

Why am I qualified to have any sort of opinion? Well, I'm
probably not. I'm technically a "relationship writer," although
I can't say the words "relationship writer" with a straight face.
(C'mon, does that even count as a job? Really? It makes me
think of the word "guru," and I hate the word "guru.") Besides,
there's an entire demographic who would tell you that I have
no idea what I'm talking about; this demographic would be my
ex-girlfriends.

But for better or worse, I'm a guy, I'm single, and I'm honest. I won't sugarcoat the male perspective, and I won't put my
gender in a falsely positive light. I did a lot of dumb things in

my twenties. I had too many flings, I collected phone numbers like baseball cards, and I hurt women I cared about. Andrea is happily married; she can show you what works. I'm not, so I can show you what doesn't. And at the very least, I'll peel back the curtain to show you what kinda-sorta-shady guys are thinking.

Before we dive in, a few words about the title. We mention this elsewhere, but I want to underscore it a thirty-seventh time—the point of this book is *not* that you should be more promiscuous. (That would be Tucker Max-ish: gross.) A dating rule of *"Always* sleep with him on the first date" would be equally absurd; actually, it's way nuttier, as it would quintuple the number of unwanted pregnancies, STDs, and men who act like pricks.

I have no idea if sleeping with him on the first date makes sense from your perspective. Maybe it does, maybe it doesn't. (In many cases, it probably doesn't—see our key disclaimers, page 39.) All I can do is give you the guy's perspective, and from the guy's perspective, if there's first-date booty, it doesn't mean that we're suddenly ready to bolt.

I told you that I'd always be honest, so here's Exhibit A: This book has very little to do with sex. The title is for shock value. A book called *The Questionable Merit of Dating Rules: Common Sense over Conventional Wisdom* just doesn't have the same sizzle.

Okay. Let's do this.

THE DATING MIND-FIELD

The rules start before you go on a single date. They affect your psychology and overall approach to romance. Some of them are explicit: "Always let the man pursue." And some of them are well-accepted bits of conventional wisdom:

- You're intimidating to men because you're too successful
- Always let the man pursue
- You find love when you're not looking
- Don't be too picky
- Men love bitches / Nice guys finish last
- Expect love at first sight

YOU'RE INTIMIDATING TO MEN BECAUSE YOU'RE TOO SUCCESSFUL

ANDREA

On *Sex and the City* Miranda had an epiphany: Mentioning her job to eligible men in a bar was a buzz kill. They would never be interested in her, because she was a lawyer. After this depressing realization, Miranda decided to approach dating differently and took on the persona of a perky stewardess at a speed-dating event. She attracted a great guy instantly and noted, "Men are threatened by good jobs. They don't want a lawyer." She unlocked the secret: men don't want to be with a successful woman.

I can't tell you how many smart and fabulous single women in Manhattan have uttered the same reason (or excuse, depending on your perspective) for why they're not dating. They've wondered if men are "intimidated" by them. A former client of mine once said, "As long as I'm in this job, I won't attract someone. Guys don't want to be with women they think are too smart."

Kind of condescending to men, no? Besides, the opposite is true. Every decade since 1939, the University of Iowa has conducted a study in which participants are asked to rank the most important qualities they want in a future mate. In the most recent study, in 2008, male participants ranked intelligence as one of the top five attractive qualities out of eighteen that a woman can

YOU'RE INTIMIDATING TO MEN BECAUSE YOU'RE TOO SUCCESSFUL

ANDREA

On *Sex and the City* Miranda had an epiphany: Mentioning her job to eligible men in a bar was a buzz kill. They would never be interested in her, because she was a lawyer. After this depressing realization, Miranda decided to approach dating differently and took on the persona of a perky stewardess at a speed-dating event. She attracted a great guy instantly and noted, "Men are threatened by good jobs. They don't want a lawyer." She unlocked the secret: men don't want to be with a successful woman.

I can't tell you how many smart and fabulous single women in Manhattan have uttered the same reason (or excuse, depending on your perspective) for why they're not dating. They've wondered if men are "intimidated" by them. A former client of mine once said, "As long as I'm in this job, I won't attract someone. Guys don't want to be with women they think are too smart."

Kind of condescending to men, no? Besides, the opposite is true. Every decade since 1939, the University of Iowa has conducted a study in which participants are asked to rank the most important qualities they want in a future mate. In the most recent study, in 2008, male participants ranked intelligence as one of the top five attractive qualities out of eighteen that a woman can

Chapter 1
THE DATING MIND-FIELD

The rules start before you go on a single date. They affect your psychology and overall approach to romance. Some of them are explicit: "Always let the man pursue." And some of them are well-accepted bits of conventional wisdom:

- You're intimidating to men because you're too successful
- Always let the man pursue
- You find love when you're not looking
- Don't be too picky
- Men love bitches / Nice guys finish last
- Expect love at first sight

own instincts. And your instincts are better than what anybody else can instruct you to do (or not do).

So why are you reading this book? Shouldn't we stop here if we believe you know best? We may not believe in hard and fast rules, but we do believe in strategies. Strategies are smart. It's helpful to have ideas on how to approach situations or dodge uncomfortable moments in your love life. Tools allow you to widen your perspective, challenge yourself, and think critically, which is always a good thing.

I hope that this book helps open your mind to new possibilities so that you can find more success in the love department (whatever *success* means to you) and that it helps guide you to listen to your best judgment over anybody else's. Choose the strategies and perspectives that resonate, and ditch the rest. My goal is to challenge the black-and-white way of thinking about dating that you've heard for years and to make dating fun again.

While rules tell you *what* to do (and when and why and where to do it), I'd rather focus on the *how*. How can you date more effectively to get closer to your goals? How can you be most authentic in your relationships? How can you quiet everybody else's wants so that you can listen to your own?

JEFF

Confession time: I'm a rule lover.

Or at least I used to be. The rules helped me flirt, they gave me a jolt of confidence, and they helped me dodge rookie mistakes. I could protect—even hide—my inner geek with rules like, "After you get her number, wait two days before calling." I wore the rules like armor.

Rules imply a world that's governed by order, logic, and reason. They appeal to our sense of gamesmanship. *If we follow the right rules, we'll win.* I liked the rules so much, in fact, that I even wrote a book about them, *The Maxims of Manhood: 100 Rules Every Real Man Must Live By.* Literally an entire book of rules, and not just any kind of rules, but the kind that you *must live by!*

And now, today, I'm saying that the rules are bunk. So how do I square this?

For one thing, the other book was mostly a joke. I don't *really* believe "Maxim 94: Your dog must be larger than a toaster." And some of the rules make plenty of sense—be yourself, don't cheat, use deodorant.

But I have three beefs with dating rules:

1. **They stamp out the nuance of human dynamics,** making everything seem as tidy as Step 1, Step 2, Step 3. Life doesn't work like that.

2. **They spawn relationship "experts"** who claim to have a bulletproof way for you to find love. It reminds me of the world of finance, pre–housing crash: talking heads spewing bad advice, like "Leverage your

mortgage. Buy a bigger home! Borrow more! He's just not that into you! Wait three days to call him back!"

3. **They don't always work.** As I've gotten older and seen more of my friends get married—seventeen weddings since '09—I've noticed one clear pattern: their happiness has nothing to do with the rules. In some cases, the woman pursued the man (a definite Don't); in others, the woman made more money than the man (gasp!); and yes, some of them hooked up on the first date. I followed the rules. They didn't. I'm still single. They're not.

This is the problem with armor: it's great for keeping you safe, but it does this by hiding your skin, dulling your senses, and keeping others at bay.

Why am I qualified to have any sort of opinion? Well, I'm probably not. I'm technically a "relationship writer," although I can't say the words "relationship writer" with a straight face. (C'mon, does that even count as a job? Really? It makes me think of the word "guru," and I hate the word "guru.") Besides, there's an entire demographic who would tell you that I have no idea what I'm talking about; this demographic would be my ex-girlfriends.

But for better or worse, I'm a guy, I'm single, and I'm honest. I won't sugarcoat the male perspective, and I won't put my gender in a falsely positive light. I did a lot of dumb things in my twenties. I had too many flings, I collected phone numbers like baseball cards, and I hurt women I cared about. Andrea is happily married; she can show you what works. I'm not, so I can show you what doesn't. And at the very least, I'll peel back the curtain to show you what kinda-sorta-shady guys are thinking.

Before we dive in, a few words about the title. We mention this elsewhere, but I want to underscore it a thirty-seventh time—the point of this book is *not* that you should be more promiscuous. (That would be Tucker Max-ish: gross.) A dating rule of "*Always* sleep with him on the first date" would be equally absurd; actually, it's way nuttier, as it would quintuple the number of unwanted pregnancies, STDs, and men who act like pricks.

I have no idea if sleeping with him on the first date makes sense from your perspective. Maybe it does, maybe it doesn't. (In many cases, it probably doesn't—see our key disclaimers, page 39.) All I can do is give you the guy's perspective, and from the guy's perspective, if there's first-date booty, it doesn't mean that we're suddenly ready to bolt.

I told you that I'd always be honest, so here's Exhibit A: This book has very little to do with sex. The title is for shock value. A book called *The Questionable Merit of Dating Rules: Common Sense over Conventional Wisdom* just doesn't have the same sizzle.

Okay. Let's do this.

On the surface, the rules are about your protection, but they have a sneaky way of making us all more insecure, less trusting, less authentic, and less likely to find a match. They breed cynicism. Gimmick-based rules like "Pretend you're busy" can help you in the short-term, but you're less likely to find long-term happiness—and yeah, we'll say it, you're less likely to find Love—by this kind of game playing. Rules like "Men love bitches" make you hide your true self. Or you could miss out on a great catch if you follow the rule "Don't talk to a man first." (Not every guy is good at approaching women, but that doesn't mean he's a lousy boyfriend.) The rules can squash your emotions—*I think I'm loving this guy, but he breaks Rule 34*—they foment doubt, and they make you wear crazy-colored glasses. Dating is supposed to be fun, but how can you be relaxed when you're counting the days between dates and the hours between calls?

You've heard some of these rules before, like "He's just not that into you," "Never date a co-worker," or *The Millionaire Matchmaker's* "No sex before monogamy." But plenty of the rules are less obvious, more subtle, and they've seeped into the dating ecosystem.

So we'll identify the rules, debate them, and show how they're actually hurting your chances. Written in (rough) chronological order, this book covers the whole spectrum of dating: the overall psychology, the first date, the men you "shouldn't" date, the awkward "this has potential" phase, seeing someone, and then rules about moving in together, engagements, or, less happily, the rules on break-ups. We'll also tackle the rules about social media,

INTRODUCTION: ON RULES

It's okay to sleep with him on the first date. It's also okay to not sleep with him on the first date. And it's okay to wait three dates, three weeks, or three years before sleeping with him.

But the old adage "If you hook up on the first date, he'll think you're a slut!" is an adage that's, well, *old*. The world has changed. For better or worse—we think better—our generation is more comfortable with sex, less prudish, and less likely to freak out after a night of boozy fun. Maybe that makes us lushes. We think it also makes us realists.

This rule—like many others—is cliché, outdated, and overly simplistic. Never trust a rule that begins with "Never," and always be suspicious of a rule that begins with "Always." The *Never* rules and *Always* rules are the accepted conventional wisdom, and the conventional wisdom is about a decade behind the curve.

The rules can hurt you.

have. (In case you're wondering, housework was ranked near the bottom at #14.) Not since the 1950s have studies supported the idea that American men don't place a high value on their mate having some smarts.

In a 2012 *New York Times* piece, writer Stephanie Coontz remarked, "Postwar dating manuals advised women to 'play dumb' to catch a man—and 40 percent of college women in one survey said they actually did so. As one guidebook put it: 'Warning!... Be careful not to seem smarter than your man.' If you hide your intelligence, another promised, 'You'll soon become the little woman to be pooh-poohed, patronized and wed.'"

My client was quoting a dating manual that was printed half a century ago, and didn't even know it.

The truth? It's actually sexy when a guy sees you as successful and smart because:

- **Your passion is sexy.** The fact that you're successful shows that you're driven, motivated, and tapped into something. Passion in life translates into passion... ahem...in other areas.
- **It's a lot of pressure for a man** to think you're going to rely on him for everything monetarily, emotionally, and otherwise. Even though a number of men like to provide, a man wants to know he's with a healthy and confident woman who isn't relying on him to "complete" her.

- **Some men *are* threatened by a woman** who appears to have her life together more than they do. But do you really want to date those men?

But while your success may not actually intimidate a potential date, successful women may scare good men away because:

- **In some cases, very successful people show little to no vulnerability.** Most dudes don't want to marry a robot.
- **Nobody likes a know-it-all.** A successful woman who puts down everything a guy says or does and corrects him (and the people around her) endlessly won't be attractive. To anybody.
- **Some women who have been competing with men in the job market for years have had to develop a thick skin,** and sometimes they forget to leave that aggressive attitude at the office. That's not to say a woman should be as demure and delicate as a flower, but she shouldn't lose her femininity just because she has to play tough at work.

Perhaps Miranda attracted her suitor not because she was a flight attendant, but because she was more attentive and playful during the speed-dating session. Smart men find smart, successful women sexy—as long as they're also accessible and fun.

JEFF

This rule reminds me of that scene in *Anchorman*, the one where Ron Burgundy hears about a female news anchor.

"What?!?! A *woman?* As an anchor?!?!" Will Ferrell roars, and then knocks over the table in fury.

That scene is funny because it's ridiculous. And this rule is funny because it's ridiculous.

Like many of the rules in this book, it might have had legs in the 70s. In the modern era—and by "the modern era," I mean post–Jimmy Carter administration—the concept of a "successful career woman" isn't some oddball novelty that perplexes men. We go to college with smart and successful women, we work with smart and successful women, and we respect smart and successful women. It's not that complicated.

Yes, there's still the occasional throwback man who wants a nice, docile, pretty doormat who will never challenge him. A real catch, right? Men (just like women) are into attractiveness, and we find success attractive.

And if the woman makes more money than the guy? Usually it's not an issue. I've dated women who have made plenty more than me (as a freelance writer, this isn't that rare). That said, things can get tricky when the woman makes *a lot* more money. Even in this case, it's not that we're "intimidated," per se, but it creates some tactical, real-world hurdles that we might or might not overcome.

Let's look at a case study.

Brooke is a lawyer. A damn good one—she just made partner. She meets a dude on OkCupid who paints circles for a living. The Circle Painter refuses to paint straight lines—his motto is, "Straight lines are artifice; circles are truth"—so there's limited demand for his work. Brooke suggests they get sushi; the Circle Painter suggests a happy hour with eight-dollar buckets of PBR. Brooke's a good sport, so she does the Pabst, and they have a good time. Date two: the Circle Painter can no longer afford the beer buckets (rough week for circles), so he suggests they take a walk in the park, where he treats her to a hot dog.

Maybe this lasts for a while. But barring a few unlikely scenarios, this relationship is doomed.

Unlikely Scenario 1:
Brooke is totally, 100 percent cool with changing her lifestyle and living like a college student again.

Unlikely Scenario 2:
Brooke is happy to pick up the bill every time they go to nice places, and more improbably, the Circle Painter is happy to let her. (Tangent: Is it silly and irrational that men feel the need to usually pay? Probably. But right or wrong, that silly and irrational mindset exists. It's also silly and irrational that we still use the electoral college, refuse to adopt the metric system, and call the previews—which come before the movie, not after—"trailers.")

Unlikely Scenario 3:
Brooke and the Circle Painter live out a romantic
comedy where true love!!! conquers this fiscal barrier.
Unlikely Scenario 4:
The demand for circles skyrockets, and the Circle Painter
gets rich.

Things don't look good for Brooke and the Circle Painter. But
this is really only an issue when the income gap is *so dramatic*
that it causes a disparity in lifestyles—it's not driven by an intimi-
dation of success.

We like successful women. Thankfully there are lots of them.

ALWAYS LET THE MAN PURSUE

ANDREA

A male hippo attracts a female by using his tail to spray her with
his feces. While that's perhaps not the most romantic way to pick
up, it's one of hundreds of examples in the wild of males trying to
secure females' attention in order to mate with them. Male frogs
make noise in an effort to elicit the females' response, male house
wrens build a nest to attract mates to nest with them, and male
turtles show off their strength and compete with other males by
stomping their feet and hovering around potential mates.

Any of this male behavior sound familiar?

Baboons are one of the few species in the animal kingdom in which the females initiate mating rituals. If a female baboon is feeling frisky, she simply has to shake her derriere to get some action. (I've seen this baboon-like behavior in bars around town.)

While we can't depend exclusively on the wild to give us insight into our human mating rituals, I do believe there is something instinctual about males pursuing females. However, as with any rule, it's not that clear-cut.

Some men—especially the shy or reserved type—appreciate when a woman takes the lead. And some men simply find it sexy when a woman pursues them.

Thirty-two-year-old Bob admitted, "I love when women pursue. It takes the pressure off of me and shows she's confident!" When I probed and asked Bob if he generally falls hard for women who make most of the advances in courtship, he paused and concluded, "I guess I haven't. But the attention from them is flattering…."

Even though the women Bob's been most attracted to allowed him to pursue them (for the most part), he still needed them to encourage him to do so by being responsive. "There's nothing worse than an icy response when you put yourself out there in dating," he said. "I won't even bother if a woman gives me attitude."

No man will put forth the effort to court a woman who he feels isn't interested. Scratch that. He may still pursue this uninterested woman and work hard to win her over with his charm and wit, but he would much prefer that a woman encourage him to keep pursuing. (Not surprisingly, men aren't big fans of rejection.)

Men are thrilled when a woman indicates interest, reciprocates affection, and acts responsively to their advances. While I do believe it's true that most men want instinctively to pursue women, a caveat to this theory is that women need to encourage the pursuit. If you're too hard to get, most self-confident guys will move on.

Courtship is awkward, exciting, and completely confusing. If it's too straightforward, it loses some of its je ne sais quoi; but if it's a roller-coaster ride full of mixed messages, cold exchanges, and standoffishness, it also doesn't work very well.

I'd be a hypocrite if I instructed you to *always* wait for a man to pursue you (I don't believe in *always* or *never* rules); but if you are generally the pursuer and want your dating luck to change, start by showing subtle interest and then let men make the next moves. These animals may be onto something....

JEFF

Things you will never hear me say:

"Damn it. The restaurant's giving us a bottle of wine . . . on the house."

"Well, this sucks. The bank just deposited five thousand dollars in my account."

"Bad news. A hot woman just approached me."

I've never understood this rule. For me the math is simple: I like women, I'm lazy, and I like it when things that I like come to me. If a woman pursues me, I'm down, assuming I'm either attracted to her or really drunk.

Of course, the word *pursue* is tricky—it can mean lots of different things. In *The Rules: Time-Tested Secrets for Capturing the Heart of Mr. Right*, Ellen Fein and Sherrie Schneider counsel "Rule 2: Don't Talk to a Man First (and Don't Ask Him to Dance)" and "Rule 3: Don't Stare at Men or Talk Too Much." In fairness, there's a lot to be said for the psychological power of withholding, so let's look at this a little closer. Specifically, there are four sub-rules on how the woman shouldn't pursue a man:

Sub-rule: Don't talk to a man first (and don't ask him to dance)

I like bold women. If she approaches me and initiates contact? Great. There's no part of me that thinks, consciously or subconsciously, *Hmm...she's hot...but I would like her more if I had to work harder.* It's true that men enjoy the chase, but the chase is not yet over. It's possible for a woman to initiate contact and still maintain a hint of intrigue.

Sub-rule: Don't stare at men or talk too much

In *The Rules*, this one begins: "Looking at someone first is a dead giveaway of interest. Let him look at *you!* If he doesn't notice you first, he's probably not interested. Keep walking; someone else will notice you." This cracks me up. If a woman so much as *looks* at us, we'll get bored and lose interest, moving on to tougher conquests. Really? Plus, here's the thing about guys: we're clueless. What you think of as a BIG SIGNAL might be lost on us completely. Sometimes you need a more aggressive pursuit just to land on our foggy radar.

Sub-rule: The woman shouldn't ask the man out on a date

Look, if I like her, I like her. If she asks me out and I'm into her? Sign me up. This doesn't mean that the woman *should* pursue or that she *must* pursue, but if she does, she's not torpedoing our chances. Like all things, of course, this has its limits. Smothering is a turnoff. And then there's this next one, the fourth category…

Sub-rule: The woman shouldn't approach the man at the bar and say, "Hey, stranger. Let's go home and fuck."

I've never been lucky enough to actually hear a woman say those words. And here's where the rule makes some sense. If it seems *too* easy, I'll get skeptical, I'll get nervous, and I'll wonder if something's wrong. Quick example: While on OkCupid, a woman messaged me and said, "This might sound forward, but I also live in Brooklyn. Wanna meet up for drinks tonight and have some fun?" Maybe it's hypocritical, maybe it's sexist, and maybe it contradicts my own philosophy, but it triggered my Spidey Sense. I didn't bite. Because you know what? If the bank deposits five thousand dollars into my account, there's probably something wrong with the transaction, and I'd be a sucker to accept it blindly.

YOU FIND LOVE
WHEN YOU'RE NOT LOOKING

JEFF

I have a complicated history with love. And it wouldn't be authentic for me to tell you how to find it. In most of this book—a dating book—I feel comfortable sharing the thoughts, fears, perspectives, anxieties, and dating strategies of men. That I can do. But the actual emotional process of falling in love? Shakier ground.

Instead, I can tell you about what I've found *not* to be helpful in finding love.

I know that *doing nothing* doesn't work. Cupid has his limits. "Love will find you!" is only partially true. If every day you go straight home from work, bunker yourself inside, and bulldoze through your Netflix queue in a ten-hour marathon, well, just *where* is love going to find you?

I know that *convincing yourself you won't find love* doesn't work. This comes dangerously close to some Tony Robbins territory—"The power of positive thinking!"—but as cynical as I am, I know that very little has been accomplished by the power of negative thinking. Pessimism can ooze into the way you think, the way you act, the way you date.

I know that *forcing yourself to love* isn't going to work. Yes, relationships take effort. But being in love shouldn't be a chore... especially in the beginning. If you feel yourself trying to love someone, you don't love them.

And I know that *you can't make a "project" of finding love.* Love is not a garden. It's not a house, it's not a tree, and it's not a new website you're launching. It's not any kind of project that you can simply design, plan, and execute. I know this because I've tried. For *Glamour* I wrote a feature called "I'm 34 and Never Been in Love." I gave myself a mission. I would force myself—through design, planning, and execution—to fall in love.

I went on lots of dates. I spoke with Science-of-Love experts like Dr. Helen Fisher. I saw a "Love Guru" (no, not at all embarrassing). I even said a "love mantra" every day (nope, not embarrassing, either). I went to an animal shelter so I could pet puppies and feel more empathy. I reread things like *Romeo and Juliet*, I listened to the Beatles nonstop for two months, and I read the love lines in my palm. I basically acted like the overly sensitive dork in a rom-com (the kind of guy I usually want to sock in the face).

The results? It's complicated. I did meet someone awesome. No, there weren't any wedding bells, and no, maybe we weren't the best fit, but we had a great relationship and I don't regret a thing. And I don't regret the Love Project.

But by the same token, it wasn't any of these "tasks" that opened me up or changed my philosophy. I didn't meet a woman—let's call her "Sarah"—through online dating or through my "Love Guru." The individual pieces didn't really matter.

What counts was the overall mindset. I shook off my cynicism, I put myself out there, and I decided that it's okay to look foolish and be vulnerable. That doesn't guarantee success or serve a magic tonic, but I'll take those chances over staying home and rewatching *The Wire*.

You often hear that you find love when you're not looking, and on some level, that's true. If you spend each day and night searching for a mate and have no interests outside of the goal to find a husband, you will most definitely emit eau de desperate. Not so sexy.

There are plenty of tales about that girl who met a great guy in the aisle of her local Rite Aid the very day she canceled her online dating profile, and about the dater who had given up completely on the male species until ... *boom!* He showed up in her life and proved good men were still available. Those stories certainly exist.

But in the years that I've covered the relationship world as a journalist, the more common stories feature women who found love once they decided to put themselves out there, rather than waiting for love to come to them. For some, this meant putting themselves out there physically (signing up for a dating site, going to new places to meet men, making their schedules more available for dating); for some, it meant taking emotional risks and challenging their perspective about their desirability or about the kind of men they should pursue for relationships. In most cases, it meant getting outside their comfort zone and away from their routine.

I've interviewed singles who eventually realized that they had put everything (career, friends, rearranging their sock drawer) ahead of what they deemed as their biggest priority—finding love. Some of these people blamed a lack of time as the reason they had stopped going out on dates, but this begs the question, *If you don't have time to date, how will you have time to be in a relationship?* Others blamed the fact that they were sick of the games, the disappointments, and the failed expectations that often accompany dating.

Dating fatigue is very real. It's easy to check out of dating after a string of less than exciting dates or disappointing relationships. The strange reality about dating is that most dates are designed to fail. In fact, that's the nature of dating! Everyone "fails" until they meet the person they want to commit to. Dating takes patience and resilience, and I'm a believer in taking a dating hiatus if you feel seriously burnt out. If you hate dating, you certainly won't be fun to hang out with on a date. Instead of forcing yourself to just get out there (as many people will advise), I'd suggest taking a little time to reconnect with your interests and focus on what makes your life meaningful and fun outside of romance.

Once you feel ready to be in a relationship, not only is expecting love to show up on your doorstep impractical (I don't know about you, but I can't recall the last time a fabulously hot man with a great sense of humor and great character randomly knocked on my front door), but taking yourself out of the driver's seat is generally not a great life approach.

Aside from taking tangible steps, you need to embrace a perspective that honors how much you have to offer and that trusts in the process of intimacy.* Once you tackle that and pair it with action, love will seek you out.

Finding love takes:

DESIRE: an innate wish for it that's coming from you, and not from your parents or peers
BELIEF: trust in the process and being open to the possibilities, even ones you don't envision

---

* If, on some secret level, you're worried about putting yourself out there because you don't feel like the great catch that you are, I challenge you to write a list of your ten best attributes. Don't be modest. If you're having a tough time acknowledging the amazing qualities you possess, enlist a good friend or a family member to help you make the list. Review this list before a date.

ACTION: putting verbs in your sentences so you aren't just talking about wanting to find love—you're actually doing something about it

If finding love is a priority, consider what you are doing—or not doing—to make that happen.

DON'T BE TOO PICKY

ANDREA

There's a joke in which a grandmother tells her single grand-daughter, "You should be with a man who adores you and treats you like a princess. You should be with a man who is smart and accomplished. You should be with a man who is charming and handsome." A moment later the grandmother adds, "Just make sure these three men don't meet."

It's fitting that the grandmother is the one who doles out advice in this joke, as so often the people closest to us express concern for our love life. They instruct us to be realistic about prospective matches and not to set our standards too high. They offer "constructive" criticism, like "You're just too picky." Keep in mind that sometimes the people who say this to you are onto something. (We'll get to that in a moment.) And sometimes they simply can't understand why you won't give their co-worker's son—you know, the one who has body odor and no sense of humor—another chance. You're both single and nice, after all!

When I was in a long-term relationship, my aunt's friend once told me that I was being too picky and asked why I didn't marry the great guy I was seeing. She reminded me that I wasn't getting any younger. (Don't you love when strangers dish out inappropriate advice?) I responded, "Thanks for your concern, but getting married is not my challenge. Staying married is my goal." (That shut her up pretty fast.)

I have no doubt that being single is a choice for you. Before you disagree, let me explain. There is always (always!) a schmuck out there somewhere, or even a really nice guy who you have no chemistry with, who would be thrilled to be with you tomorrow. But that's not what you're looking for—and I don't blame you.

On the other hand, sometimes you *are* being too particular and critical in dating. You know more than anyone does if your best friend or even your grandmother is right when she points out that you're being *too picky.* Be honest with yourself. Do you rarely like any guy that you meet? If you find you're generally negative when you meet new men, and your inner voice is constantly criticizing everything about the way a guy dresses, speaks, or moves, it may be worth making a commitment to give people you meet more of a chance before dismissing them.

If you are being too picky, there could be a number of reasons why. It could be a defense mechanism, since it's easier to push people away and reject them before they reject you. Ironically, low self-esteem causes some of us to reject people, because we don't really believe they'd like us. Or perhaps you have healthy self-esteem and know that you offer amazing qualities in a relationship, so you don't want to settle. Perhaps you're proud to be picky.

I don't believe you should settle when you settle down. I think you should be extremely picky, but make sure your pickiness is guided by qualities that are truly important to you in a partner. Being picky about the shoes a guy wears or what part of town he lives in is potentially cutting you off from someone who may be a great match. These superficial things hardly matter in a long-term partnership.

Be picky about the things that matter. Be picky about the way he treats you and the way you feel around him. You shouldn't settle for less than being attracted to, excited by, and genuinely interested in a person you're going to spend a tremendous amount of time with. That kind of pickiness is nonnegotiable.

JEFF

Unless you're chewing up guys for Seinfeldy reasons—"She has man-hands, George, man-hands!"—it's almost impossible to be too picky.

Being picky means that you know what you want. You're unwilling to settle.

Being picky means that you have good self-worth. You have exacting standards because you deserve it, damn it.

Being picky means that you're comfortable being single. You have fun with your friends, your family, yourself. Someday you'll be in a happy monogamous relationship, but until the right guy comes along, why force it?

Being picky means, by definition, that you pick well. Sure, it might have taken you a long time to look at the menu—and maybe you asked the waiter some annoying questions about the tofu—but now that you've ordered, you're less likely to send the dinner back.

Being picky means that you live in the 21st century, not the 19th. In geological terms, being picky is a very recent phenomenon. Let's enjoy it. We used to have little choice in who we married: maybe it was determined by our parents, or maybe you could choose only from the seven boys in your village, and you certainly had to be done picking by the time you were 21. (You had children to pump out! Enough dawdling!)

Being picky means that you're saving the best for last. So take your time.

Signed,
A too-picky guy who's still single
(So make of this what you will)

MEN LOVE BITCHES /
NICE GUYS FINISH LAST

ANDREA

Here's the issue I have with the very popular theory that men love bitches and nice guys finish last: it is essentially (and quite literally) encouraging people to mistreat each other. Aside from the fact that this idea puts negative karma out into the dating and mating world, the rule is counterproductive. Kindness consistently ranks as one of the most important qualities one seeks in a prospective mate.

Psychologist and author Daniel Goleman has written about how our brains are actually hardwired to look for kind people in all our relationships, since we respond in kind (excuse the pun) when we interact with nice folks. Seeing someone smile triggers a smile response in your brain. And if you're around someone who is in a bad mood or who is mean-spirited, I'm sure you've experienced that same emotion. It's amazing how much our moods and brains mirror emotions. For this reason, I cut people with "negative energy" out of my life a few years ago. Time is precious, and I'd rather not waste it with Debbie (or Doug) Downer.

Aside from the fact that it's generally nicer to hang out with nice people, most healthy people are attracted to generosity and good character. Part of the mating process is about finding that guy or gal you want to raise babies with. You want your partner to be strong and attractive, but you also want him to be caring and reasonable in this role.

The reason I point to the fact that healthy people like good character is that I assume that's who you are (or want to be) and that's who you want to attract. The reality is that a jerk may attract a woman who hasn't developed enough self-confidence to recognize that she deserves better, or a bitchy woman may get the guy who she will eventually lose respect for because he is such a pushover.

What people generally mean when they say they're not attracted to "nice" people is that they're not attracted to people who are boring or weak, but boring or weak is not synonymous with nice.

I've rarely heard anyone say, "I don't like the person I'm dating, because he's thoughtful" or "I don't like her, because she listens to what other people have to say and is caring...."

You may attract a mate if you give him attitude, but is that really someone you want to be with over the long term? Is this someone who brings out your best self? Probably not.

I don't love bitches.
Rule debunked.
Done.

Fine, okay, I'll elaborate.

This crazy rule is built on some not-crazy psychology, so let's unravel the nonsense. It rests on the premise that we, as humans, pursue that which retreats from us, so logically, we should retreat, we should withhold, and we should act "bitchy" so others will pant and drool.

This can work in the short-term. Tactics like not calling him back, showing up late for dates, and blowing him off could, potentially, have the intended effect, just like how you can trick a dog by hiding his dinner.

But there are a few problems with this strategy. First, as Andrea said, do you really want to date a man who loves bitches? You deserve a guy who loves you without the gimmicks. Second, if you hoodwink a guy with these clever deceits, how will you know if he's truly into you, or if he's just a puppet dancing on your strings? My memory of Pinocchio is a little rusty, but when the puppets notice those strings, they're no longer content, right?

Third, just think about the converse. Men could theoretically take the same hard line and say, "Nice guys finish last" and "Women love assholes!" and then act like one, hoping that a cold, calculating approach will make the ladies swoon. And maybe some will. Let's see how those couples are doing five years from now. Or what if we applied Kant's Categorical Imperative, which states, "Act only according to that maxim whereby you can, at the same time, will that it should become a universal law." In other words, what if everyone acted like this? What if all women acted like bitches and all men acted like assholes? (This world exists. It's called high school.)

One important disclaimer. To the extent that this rule uses the word *bitch* just to be provocative, and that the theory is actually, at heart, about how a woman should be strong, independent, empowered, and self-sufficient, well, I'm all for that. Who isn't? But the word describing that kind of behavior is not bitch. It's woman. And lots of men are into them.

Do Men Love Bitches, and Do Nice Guys Finish Last?

"It's all about confidence. Jerks do well with women because they give off an air of not caring. And that is easily confused with confidence. But confident, nice guys can do just as well as jackasses. The same goes for women." —Scott

"Nice guys who allow themselves to be doormats finish last. Proper gentlemen who do the right thing, have respect for both themselves and for women might not finish first or last, but they finish *right*." —Ross

"Women love bitches: true! I think men like women who are unattainable." —Diana

"I think that's what 'less than' nice guys say to give themselves an excuse not to look at themselves as the source of their aloneness." —Cynthia

"I've seen some of the sweetest guys marry the biggest bitches. I think the men like 'working for it' and trying to please these women!" —Renata

"I don't think men love bitches. I think women who can attract a lot of guys are a little more free to express their true bitchiness." —Matt

"I think both men and women want a 'nice' partner. The reason why those myths exist is that the 'nice guy/woman' tends to show less confidence and 'look' less attractive, while the jerk/bitch always looks (over)confident and attracts more." —Amparo

"I'll always be a nice guy, and *no*, I don't like bitches." —Daniel

"I personally would never marry a bitch. I find women who act like 'bitches' are a bit aggressive and are doing so to mask something underneath…. The best relationships are without games and employ honest communication, instead of manipulation. Nice guys *finish*, and guys love *ex*-bitches." —Alex

"Those myths arise from youth. Young people are all about excitement, and arrogance is easily mistaken for confidence. In matters of love and attraction we must all evolve and learn on our own what qualities are important in a mate, as well as honestly examining what qualities we wish to offer." —Travis

"There's a lot of reverse causality here. Guys who finish last are 'nice' in part because they didn't have a chance to do otherwise. If you never get laid, then you don't have many chances to break hearts and act like a jerk." —Max

"Confidence is attractive. Both in men and women. You can be nice and confident, but many people get confused here. Nice, wimpy guys will say that they always finish last because they're nice. They finish last because they're wimpy. Same theme for the men-liking-bitches theory: Bitch is bad. Confident is good." —Adam

"I don't know about those theories, but I personally live by 'Ditch the bitch. Make the switch.'" —Sean (who's gay)

EXPECT LOVE AT FIRST SIGHT

JEFF

You should know this much at first sight: whether you want to rip their clothes off. That's not unimportant. That physical spark can carry you through the tough times, the grown-up times, the sober times that feel like a Raymond Carver short story.

This physical attraction is a necessary, but not sufficient criteria. How about your actual "chemistry"? Some people just *click* right away. But what if you don't have that instant connection? Are you doomed?

You're not, since Love at First Sight has two Achilles' heels: false positives and false negatives.

False positives

First encounters are easy to fake. Maybe *fake* is too harsh a word; it's more accurate to say that you can "coast by on a cocktail of charm, questions, and expository dialogue." First conversations are easy. You talk about where you're from, what you do, how you like your neighborhood, the usual nuts and bolts of getting-to-know-you. The words can flow and even gush. You probably have some canned stories—even if you don't realize it—about the funny time you fell asleep on the subway and woke up in the Bronx. As these words (and alcohol) flow, it's easy to feel, *Yes, we totally click. This person gets me*. Then the second date rolls around and you realize that the verbal well is dry; you have nothing to talk about.

Sometimes the false positive is intentional. He might be a player who can flick on the charm for two hours and then, after you've fooled around, unleash his inner douche. Note: This is the risk—or one of the many risks (see page 39)—of sleeping with him on the first date.

And of course, there's the obvious "relationshipy" stuff: Do you share the same values? Have compatible-ish goals in life? Like thick- or thin-crust pizza?

False negatives

Not everyone's a craaazy-fun-extrovert who clicks right away. Some people take time. Maybe they seem kinda boring in the first few minutes, but then, once they open up, they're a firecracker. And some people are just *not good at dating*. Dating can be awkward and weird and stressful. Look, you're attractive, and maybe the guy's nervous when he meets you, and he stumbles and bumbles his way through the first glass of wine. Then maybe he'll relax, slow down, and turn out to be the best boyfriend since Lloyd Dobler. Or maybe he's an introverted serial killer. Who knows! This is the joy and the curse of dating. You never really know . . . especially at first sight.

ANDREA

If all happily married women embraced this rule, they wouldn't have met their matches. There was Jen, who spent her whole blind date with her (now) husband trying to figure out who else she could set him up with. And Esther, who was interested in her husband's friend when she met them both at a party. Both of these women thought the guys they met were perfectly nice and good—for someone else.

Complete disclosure: I'm one of the women who married a guy who wasn't my type (at all!). During the first few minutes of meeting my husband, Michael, I thought he was a little pushy and presumptuous. When we met, Michael found a way to steal my number by sending himself a text message from my phone (slick). He continued to follow up almost daily to see when we could hang out again. I found him a little too eager, but he made me laugh, so I occasionally gave in. We developed a close friendship, but he wasn't my type, so I didn't consider him to be a romantic possibility.

Michael would tell you now that he knew if he stuck around long enough, I'd eventually come around and realize he was a good match. (See? He's presumptuous!) He was right, of course. However, had I followed the rule "You should know right away if he's a match!" I would never have opened my mind and heart to the possibility of being with my husband, who is a much better match for me than the men I had previously been instantly attracted to.

The reality is that on a first date, you don't need to know if you are going to marry someone. In fact, I hope you *don't* know that right away, since you'll be basing it on a superficial impression. A first date is a first meeting. You're there simply to learn a little about a new person and to see if you should spend time learning a little more.

Here's my disclaimer: If you are completely annoyed or bored by someone and feel like doing your taxes would be seriously more interesting and sexy than another date with a certain dude, don't give him another chance. You don't need to know on the first date that someone is your lifelong match, but if you have a visceral reaction that screams, "I never want to see him again!" or "I'm grossed out by this person!" don't ignore that, either. But open your mind to the possibility that sometimes a first date is awkward or uncomfortable, and you may not know if someone is a match for you instantly.

My first-date litmus test to assess if you want to go out again is to ask yourself (not out loud), *Am I having fun with this person?*

Am I curious to learn more? Stop there. Stop your mind from wandering to *Could I really have babies with this man?*

Chapter 2
THE FIRST DATE

The first date is littered with rules. You must do this and not do that. Wear this, never say this, and for goodness' sake, always blah, blah, blah. How about just enjoying yourself?

- Never sleep with him on the first date
- Always let the man pay
- Wear a dress (and heels) on the first date
- Go to dinner on the first date
- Never talk about politics or religion on the first date
- Make a perfect first impression

NEVER SLEEP WITH HIM ON THE FIRST DATE

ANDREA

A 36-year-old friend called me, crying, last year. She went out on a fantastic date with a great guy. "But…," she sobbed, "I ruined it! We slept together!"

I asked her about the rest of the date. Did they get along, have an interesting conversation, laugh together? "Yes, we had a really good connection. That's the problem!"

Problem?

When it comes to how long you should wait until you sleep with him, here are some of the popular rules I've heard: "Don't sleep with him until monogamy" (Patti Stanger, *The Millionaire Matchmaker*). "Don't sleep with him until he's said 'I love you'" (*The Rules*). "Don't sleep with him until you're out of this house" (my dad).

None of these rules served me very well when I was single, and they don't serve the singles I've worked with over the years. Putting arbitrary timelines around intimacy makes most of us live in our heads and takes us out of the experience of being with someone and letting our connection unfold organically (or orgasmically, as the case may be).

For as many times as I've heard the advice to wait x number of months before having sex, I've heard stories of women and men who have successfully found love and partnership following a first-date hookup. I can disprove the "Never sleep with him on the first date" rule by referencing a number of these people — including my friend mentioned above, who dated the guy for four months after she cried to me — but I'd rather use logic. The average dater does not wait to start her life, focus on her career, or have sex until after she settles down. Some women actively seek out sex with no strings attached. Times have changed since this rule was created. Few men I've interviewed lose respect for or interest in a woman they're into because they slept with her too soon. And the ones who do . . . do you really want to date them?

The strategy/case for waiting

When men and women have sex, they release oxytocin, a hormone that makes them feel attached to someone (oxytocin is often referred to as the "cuddle hormone" and is also released when a woman breast-feeds her baby). While it's true that men also release oxytocin following an orgasm, women and men respond differently to the production of the hormone. Estrogen and oxytocin make a woman feel close and comforted, whereas testosterone mutes oxytocin's nurturing effects. So if you know that you're going to start fantasizing about having his babies after a hot make-out session, it may be a good idea *not* to have sex on a first date.

For those of you who would rather wait to sleep with a guy, more power to you. I'm not saying that one should never wait to have sex with a man she likes. If your instinct is to hold off, because you recognize that sleeping with your crush won't bring out the best in you and may sabotage your chance for a good relationship, follow your gut.

Part of the courtship dance is the pursuit and the intrigue. Sometimes waiting to have sex with someone you really like can enhance the excitement and build up healthy tension . . . and that can be really fun.

But consider that you can still build excitement and anticipation after you've seen each other naked. The promise of sex is hardly the only thing a guy needs in order to pursue you. In my friend Jason's words, "I don't lose interest if we hook up early. I lose interest if I sense she's controlling or needy. . . . "

Oftentimes the things we think are deal breakers in dating aren't really the criteria guys are using to decide if they're into us.

Some people will tell you not to sleep with him too early because "Why buy the cow if he can get the milk for free?" Note that the person offering this advice to you is insinuating that you are a cow. . . .

The bottom line is that if you want to sleep with a man after a great first date, follow your *wants* and not your (or other people's) *shoulds*. Living by shoulds is a great recipe for dissatisfaction . . . and I guarantee it won't make the dating process very fun.

JEFF

Why not? Besides the risk of herpes, pregnancy, and losing the respect of your partner, what could possibly go wrong? Kidding. Mostly. There's obviously no one right or wrong answer. It's okay to sleep with him, it's okay not to sleep with him, and it's okay to wait three dates or three months or until you get married. (Note to future girlfriend: please don't wait until we get married.) Instead of saying what I think the woman should do or shouldn't do, let's clear up some misconceptions about how the average guy feels about first-date sex.

We all know the classic take: if the woman "gives it up" too soon, the guy, having found the hidden treasure, will lose interest and pivot to his next conquest. At a casual glance, this seems like a reasonable theory. We do like to chase. And the forbidden fruit is desired because it's forbidden, not because it's fruit.

There's just one counter to this theory, and it's simple: if the man and the woman are a match, it doesn't really matter when they have sex. If it's meant to be, it's meant to be. If they're compatible in terms of chemistry, shared values, and a mutual fondness for 17th-century gargoyles, then a hookup won't sink the relationship. And if the guy *does* freak-out, lose interest, or not call afterwards? This would have (probably) happened eventually.

But here's an even more honest truth about men: we don't really think about it.

In the history of the planet Earth, this exchange has never happened:

Matt: She's awesome, dude.
Steve: Yeah?
Matt: She's smoking hot. She's funny. She even likes
       Voltron. There's only one little problem.
Steve: She's not smart?
Matt: It's not that. She's a doctor.
Steve: She's married?
Matt: Nah.
Steve: She has a third nipple? What is it? Tell me!
Matt: We had sex on the first date.
Steve: Oh. Matt, I'm so sorry.
Matt: Yeah. It sucks.
Steve: What a shame.
Matt: Yep. There was potential.
Steve: Deal breaker.
Matt: Definitely. Back to the drawing board.

We're simple creatures. This is how our mind works: We see a pretty girl. We have fun with pretty girl. We kiss pretty girl. We want to sleep with pretty girl.

That's it. That's about as far as we get in our analysis. We don't think, "This one's Girlfriend Material because she waited a month, and that one's Booty-call Material because she came back to my place." You either have chemistry or you don't. True, waiting can amplify the intrigue and the desire, but the *mere act of waiting* does not magically create chemistry. Waiting does not make us say, "Now, *that's* the kind of woman I could marry!"

That said . . .

There's plenty of merit in waiting. (If I have a daughter twenty-five years from now—God help me—I would counsel her to wait; then again, I would also counsel her to join a nunnery.) We get it. Waiting helps you weed out the creepers, waiting lowers risk, waiting helps establish trust, and waiting can bring delayed gratification, which is hot. And waiting has a certain old-fashioned courtship charm. As my friend Kerry says, "No, it's not wrong to sleep with someone on the first date. But if you actually like the person and want a future together, there will be plenty of time to fuck (or make love), and waiting will not only be a foundation for a strong relationship, but will also be a sweet ache to reminisce about much later."

So no one's arguing that you *should* hook up on the first date. But if you decide to, don't worry, we're not going to spend seventeen hours with our buddies, discussing how it impacts our feelings. We're not going to think less of you. By definition, that would mean we'd need to think less of ourselves, right, unless we're complete hypocrites?

We'll think, *Sex. Cool.* And we'll probably want to do it again.

Should You Have Sex on the First Date?

"I wouldn't judge a woman at all if we slept together on the first date. I really enjoy my memories of sex on the first date and see it as a sign that we really clicked, not as a sign that she's somehow a bad person." —Mark

"I decided to seduce Phil because he was visiting from out of town and therefore there would be no strings attached. The next morning I realized that he was actually lovely, thoughtful, and interesting. He even held my hand on the way to Starbucks. We spent the next year dating long distance, and six months ago he moved to Toronto and into my apartment. It was one successful one-night stand!" —Rica
Update: Rica and Phil are now engaged.

"If the moment feels right, and there's chemistry, why not sleep together? Most women that I've dated, I've slept with on the first date. There have also been many women that I've had sex with on a first date that I never went out with again. If I really like someone, whether or not I've slept with them already is not going to matter…." —Teddy

"I say do what feels right or what you think is right. I basically slept with one of my favorite boyfriends on the first date, and I never regretted it." —Amanda

"Embarrassingly, I slept with my future husband on date number two…didn't really want to, but he was persistent, and it somehow ended up working out. I'm not totally proud of that fact, but it is the truth. Actually, I don't really care at this point. It seems to be working out (going on six years!)." —Alix

"Every great love I've had started with a one-night stand…and ended in a relationship." —Jonathan

"If you both feel like your relationship may not progress beyond a booze-fueled first date, why not at least get laid?" —Eddie

"Here's the thing. If someone is going to judge you for sleeping with them on the first date—something they were doing, too, might I say—do you really want to be with that type of person who lives by such double standards? I wouldn't. That said, know yourself and know if sleeping with someone changes the game plan for you—especially if you're looking for something serious. If you tend to obsess over everyone you have sex with, whether or not you've known them for two hours or two months, maybe hold off. Same goes if you have a history of falling head over heels quickly for the wrong person. You'll need your wits about you, and sex can change that." —Amy

"Yes. And we're getting married in the fall." —Ali

Disclaimers: When you really shouldn't hop into bed on Date One

As we've said before (and as we'll say again), it's okay *not* to sleep with him on the first date. And many times it would be crazy, suicidal, unwise, unhealthy, or criminal. We trust you to use your judgment. But just ~~to appease our lawyers~~ for fun, let's look at some scenarios where it clearly doesn't make sense:

You're underage

This is not a book for teenagers. We're assuming you are an adult and have been dating for a while. (Helpful tip: You're not our audience if you still have Bieber Fever.)

You're a virgin

North America doesn't manufacture enough shotguns for all the fathers who would hear about our book, track us down, and kill us in cold blood. So let's be clear: If you are a virgin, do not sleep with him on the first date. And give this book to someone else. (Also, stay in school, don't do drugs, use sunscreen, and make regular backups of your computer files.)

You have moral/religious reasons for waiting

We respect that. And we would never suggest that you change your values. We're not preachers. If you want to wait a week or a year or until you're married—for whatever reason—we're behind you 100 percent.

You're sloshy, falling-down drunk

When you've slammed your fourth tequila shot, knocked over the bar stool, and belted out an entire rendition of "Sweet Caroline," maybe, just maybe, it's a bad idea to let a complete stranger into your bedroom.

You feel that you'll become too emotionally involved too soon

Many women have said this to us: They don't have a moral problem with hooking up on the first date, but they worry that it will affect *them*. They prefer to take things slow, as it keeps things on an even keel as the relationship progresses. Makes sense.

You have an STD

Enough said.

You're not being safe

Nope, we're not counting the "hope method" as effective birth control and disease prevention.

You sense that the guy is kind of shady

Trust your instincts. He probably is.

You feel that you "owe" the guy

You don't owe him anything physical. Ever. It doesn't matter how nice or generous he was on your date. He could have bought you roses, hired a private helicopter, whisked you to Cape Cod for the world's finest oysters, and then popped a bottle of champagne that was given to him as a personal gift by George Stephanopoulos. It doesn't matter. If you're not into the dude, you owe him nothing physical, zilch, nada, not even a kiss.

ALWAYS LET THE MAN PAY

JEFF

There are plenty of dumb rules. This is not one of them. On the first date, yes, the man should always pay.

It's not because we think the woman can't pay or won't pay. There's no hidden undercurrent. We get that you're independent, self-sufficient, and are perfectly capable of buying your own martinis. So why do we insist on paying? Because every once in a long, long while, we like to behave in a way that makes us feel like we're not assholes.

The guy should pay even if he's broke. The guy should pay even if the date wasn't his idea. The guy should pay even if halfway through the date, he decides he's not interested. The guy should pay even if the *woman* clearly isn't interested.*

Why do we feel so strongly about this? The exact roots of this maxim in particular, and of chivalry in general, are tough to pinpoint. All I know is that for 99.99999 percent of men, the motivation is coming from a good place. We don't hold the door because we think you can't open it; we do it because it's good manners. We don't offer to carry a heavy package because

---

* Yes. Even if you decide that you loathe the guy and that you would never peck him on the cheek, much less swap saliva, even then, yes, he should pay, and he shouldn't begrudge you a thing. These are the risks of dating. We don't have an "I'll buy her drinks only if she makes out with me" policy. And the ass-hats that do? They deserve to lose some bread.

we think you're feeble; we do it because it's polite. Same with offering to pay on the first date. And the guy who *doesn't pay* isn't some daring, trailblazing pioneer for women's rights; he's just cheap.

Things tend to even out. There are plenty of "external costs" to a first date that men can't fathom. To get ready for a date, all the guy needs is a clean shirt, a comb, and a well-hidden condom. Women? Skin care! Shoes! Makeup! Hair appointments! Small little tubes of weird gel that somehow cost fifty-seven dollars! These are the external costs, and women bear more of them than men. So it's only fair that we take care of Date Number One.

As for dates two, three, four, and beyond? Here I'm less of an absolutist. Other issues come into play—relative incomes, the types of activities, and who suggested the date itself. Most guys are happy to pay more often than not, but if the woman *never* offers, then it's a turnoff. It doesn't have to do with the money (well, it kind of does); it has to do with a sense of entitlement. And it can't be a fake offer or a "go-for-the-purse-in-slow-motion" offer; she needs to actually pay for something. Even if it's just a token, even if it's just coffee, even if it's just the cab ride home.

ANDREA

A few summers ago I interviewed two hundred women in Manhattan and posed the question, "Would you go on a second date with a man if he didn't offer to pay for your first date?" The answer was an overwhelming "Hells No!"

Some women, especially women under 30 or those who were from another country, said they didn't expect men to pay for them. One woman remarked, "It's too much pressure for him to pay for me if I don't even know if I'm into him yet." When it comes to who should pay for a first date, these women prefer an egalitarian approach. But they're in the minority.

One woman I spoke with decided that she was over a guy, someone whom she was initially attracted to, when he let her pay. The coffee bill came to $4.82, and since she had only a ten-dollar bill, she put it on the table and apologized for not having smaller bills. She expected her date to say, "Don't be silly!" and push her ten-dollar bill back, but he took it. And then didn't give her the change. "He made money on our date!" she said and laughed. Needless to say, she had no interest in going out with him on a second date.

There are even some women who not only expect a man to pay for dates, but also see dating as a good business model: free drinks and lavish meals! (These scheming women aren't you, of course!) Take this 23-year-old woman, who goes under the alias Minerva McGonagall and who admitted to *Business Insider* last year that she used sites like Match.com to score nice dinners around Manhattan. She said that online dating in New York helped her curb her mounting debt. Meanwhile, she may have put some nice men in debt because of this approach....

Then there's the dating rule that discourages women from reaching for their wallets or offering to pay on a date since "that will set a bad precedent." This rule is especially ridiculous. Men appreciate when a woman offers to chip in and graciously accepts his chivalrous efforts, rather than assuming the tab will be taken care of. If you never offer to pay or assume the man will always pick up the check (especially after a few dates), you might come off as entitled and spoiled, not to mention terribly old-fashioned.

While it's true that most women would like a man to pay on a first date, there are exceptions to this "rule." Here are a few scenarios in which it may make more sense for you to pay for the first date or split the bill:

- If you asked him out
- If you want to send a clear message that you're not interested in him romantically
- If he ordered a 7UP and you got beef bourguignon

Should the Man Always Pay on a First Date?

"The feminists will hate me here, but yes. I have a good job, I'm independent, and I can pay my own bills. I probably make more money than some guys I go out with (that says more about their salaries than mine—it's a low bar). But if I go on a first date and the guy doesn't pay, I walk away thinking that he's not interested, that he's not generous/caring, and it somehow, oddly, also makes me feel less feminine and attractive. The date also seems less fun somehow. Blame nature. Blame nurture, whatever." —Amy

"Gender has nothing to do with who should pay on a first date.... It should be the person that asks for a date. Traditionally, the man asks, but if a woman asks, then she's on the hook. Of course, I'd still like her to make a gesture or reach for the bill, just so it's not assumed that I'll pay and so she doesn't seem like a mooch." —Kevin

"Girls are usually comfortable around me on a first date, so when I offer to pay for dinner, they usually offer to buy drinks at the next bar, which is usually a good sign that they're interested in me." —Teddy

"Even as a man-loving feminist who encourages my lady friends to be independent creatures, I (cringe) have to say yes. A dude paying on the first date is a subtle acknowledgment of traditional roles. The sensitive, modern, totally evolved guys that I know and love still value being able to take care of a lady, and most women, no matter how strong and independent they are, want to know that they're with someone who can hold their own." —Monica

"If you are remotely interested in her, or you expect to continue to run into her in the future, then the cost-benefit analysis is clear. The upside of splitting the bill is exactly half of the bill. The downside is potentially much greater." —Matt

"If a woman doesn't offer to pay for something, anything, at any point during the first three dates, it's a turnoff." —David

WEAR A DRESS (AND HEELS) ON THE FIRST DATE

ANDREA

Patti Stanger told Today.com that men don't like "red hair, curly hair, and print dresses" (random combination, I agree). According to Ms. Stanger, "The only men who like redheads are Irish."

I hope none of you red-haired beauties or sexy curlys would change your hair to satisfy this ridiculous dating rule, especially since I know a number of men who are most drawn to women with curly or red hair. (And I'm sure there are those who love red, curly hair!)

Of course, your appearance matters in dating. You're less likely to attract a dude if you look like me when I wake up in the morning, but there's no one rule on how to look on a date other than this one from my friend Joe: "Look hot!" He adds, "But still approachable..."

Conventional wisdom says you should be dolled up and perfectly pretty on a date. While it's nice to look good, make sure you don't look so made up and coiffed that a guy thinks he can't have fun with you. If you look untouchable, a man is less likely to think about...well, touching you.

Lady in red

There are theories about the colors that attract men, and in fact there's some evidence to support the idea that men react differently to women when they wear red. An article in the *Journal of Experimental Social Psychology* describes how researchers showed men a photo of a woman wearing a white T-shirt and a copy of the same photo, which had been doctored so that the woman appeared to be wearing the same shirt in red. The question posed to the men was, "How keen is this woman to romance?" (Read "sex.") The guys measured the woman's attitude about and interest in sex about 1 to 1.5 points higher when she was wearing the red shirt. So if you want to be a little more flirty, try wearing a nice shade of red or crimson. But don't sweat it. If you look good and wear a flattering cut, you can wear a shower-curtain print and he'll still think you're hot.

What not to wear

Steer clear of oversize, baggy clothes that make you look shapeless or like an old woman who lives in a shoe. And avoid tight, shiny, short, and low cut combined. It's too much! Sexy is hinting at your assets, not showing them all.

Other than that, wear (almost) anything that you feel good in. Call attention to your face or to the parts of your body that you love. Love your legs? Show them off in a short skirt. Love your curves? Accentuate them in something a little low cut or clingy. It sounds pretty obvious, but it's amazing how many of us try to wear trends that don't really work for our bodies (and don't make us feel great, as a result).

Ms. Stanger also suggests showing cleavage and wearing a dress at every opportunity. You may feel a little out of place at a baseball game in your dress and heels, so use discretion and dress for the occasion. That said, there's a nugget of truth in this *Millionaire Matchmaker* rule—you're a woman, and your date apparel should reflect that. In other words, it's not very sexy when your date realizes he has the same big button-down shirt at home.

I know less about women's fashion than I do about the economy of Bangladesh. For example, I don't understand the difference between a shirt and a blouse. I can't understand the popularity of Uggs. And I'll never understand why a beautiful woman would wear oversize sunglasses—in the shape of two stop signs—that conceal 80 percent of her face.

So take this all with a grain of salt. That said, I can break down different colors, outfits, looks, and, since Andrea once asked me, "What do men think about too much cleavage?" I'll tackle that one, too:

The color red

According to the study Andrea cited, I am 37 percent more likely to marry a woman if she's wearing red. (Or maybe I misread things. I was laughing too hard to read the exact quote.) These studies are bonkers. If a woman looks good, then she looks good, period.

Crazy cleavage

So frickin' awesome…if I'm staring at it in my bedroom or, more likely, on my computer screen. Look, I'm as progressive as they come, but if my date rolls up in some deep, nippley V-neck that would make Kim Kardashian look modest? Actually…that still sounds kind of awesome, and my reaction would probably be, *Now I really want to sleep with her.* But! Then I'll think some more. And when the cleavage-buzz wears off, maybe I'd wonder if I should take her less seriously. Maybe.

Hint of cleavage

Sure. That's nice.

No cleavage

Who cares? There are millions of ways that a woman can entice. If a woman rolls up in a conservative shirt (or blouse?) that doesn't reveal any curves ... *it doesn't matter.* Thanks to *Maxim*; *SI*'s swimsuit issue; just about every men's magazine, website, porno, music video, or commercial ever created, you get the impression that all of us men are Neanderthals who, without the company of females, grunt around, chanting "Breasts! Breasts! Breasts!" We do that only some of the time. Attractive is attractive. It doesn't matter if it's showy or not showy, curvy or not curvy.

And on that note ...

That's kind of it.

I tried to make a long list of the different types of outfits that women wear in order to tell you what guys tend to think. Dress vs. jeans? Makeup vs. non-makeup? Skirt vs. shorts? I started to make this list, but I had a hard time writing it, and then I realized there's a reason. I don't have an opinion on these things, because *it just doesn't matter.*

Unless the guy works in the fashion industry, he's not going to think about your outfit and triple-guess your choices. This is about as nuanced as he'll get: *she looks hot.* Sure, I understand that your choices in apparel could impact how you appear, which, in turn, could influence the guy's reaction, but it's just not something we think about.

One more thing. Hey, Patti? I like redheads, curly hair, and print dresses, as well as non-redheads, straight hair, and non-print dresses.

GO TO DINNER ON THE FIRST DATE

ANDREA

Back to Ms. Stanger. She's stated that "Coffee is cheap, drinks are an audition, lunch is an interview, but dinner means business, the business of romance." She insists that her clients treat their dates to expensive meals and encourages them to book over-the-top outings, like a private jet ride or his and her massages, to add to the date experience.

If I were on a first date with someone I didn't really like and had to sit through hours of dinner conversation and a luxurious outing, I'd feel like it was a waste of time for me and my date, and certainly a waste of money. This fancy first-date rule does daters a disservice—it's too much pressure for all.

I agree with Patti that coffee on a first date should be skipped, but the reason to avoid Starbucks isn't that it's "cheap," but that it's forgettable. It's harder to have the potential for a romantic spark with your date if the lighting is fluorescent, coffee machines are rattling, and people are competing with you to grab a table. Then again, some cafés are charming and romantic, in which case it's a wonderful idea for a first date.

I generally suggest that daters plan a happy hour outing for date one. The prices are reasonable (we shouldn't evaluate someone based on how much money he spends on a date—especially

Q: What if I don't drink?

If you don't want to go for a drink on a first date, consider sharing an experience, like going to the park and getting ice cream in nice weather, or playing a round of pool at a neighborhood pub on a cool day. An activity date is generally memorable, and trying something new together will help create a bond. (As a bonus, most men are more likely to open up more while doing something active.) And even if your date isn't a match, at least you'll have fun or have an interesting experience.

if the date is creative!), the vibe is usually fun, and there's a hard beginning and end time built into the experience. Happy hour is usually held between 4 and 7 p.m., so you can meet your date after work and skip off to your (fake) dinner plans after that. Or if your happy hour date is going well, you can always transition to dinner with him.

It's been suggested that as much as 70 percent of our communication is relayed through our body language. Flirting cues are more likely to be exchanged over a drink than over a sandwich or a cup of coffee. We not only collect subtle information on our date's interests by observing body language, but we also can communicate our own with nonverbal cues. Stroking the stem of a wineglass or swirling your finger around the rim of a martini glass or a beer mug is generally a sign that you want to touch the person you are seated across from. Most of these nonverbal cues don't happen consciously, of course. (There's nothing less sexy than trying to act sexy!)

JEFF

I'll give it this: dinner isn't the *worst* first-date idea. It's not even in the bottom ten. Here are just a few activities that are even worse:

- Cleaning your toilet bowl
- Returning a cable box to Time Warner
- Window shopping at jewelry stores
- Couple's visit to the dermatologist
- Coffee*

See? These are all worse than dinner, which is problematic for at least 376 different reasons. Here are a few:

#37 You have no escape
If you don't like the dude, you suffer through a gauntlet of appetizers, drinks, entrées, and awkwardly waiting for the check. It's the longest two hours since *The Tree of Life*.

---

* Coffee. Coffee is something you do with your visiting aunt, a co-worker, or a friend that you don't really like. It's the pits. You take a tense, awkward situation to begin with, and you add caffeine, a stimulant? Smart. There's only one time where coffee on a date is appropriate: the next morning.

#102 Geography

The geography of a bar is fluid: it lets you rearrange the seating as the body language evolves. At dinner, you're usually seated across from each other, which is also the way you sit in a job interview, which is also the way that Jack Bauer, during an interrogation, sits across from a terrorist.

#9 Stomachs

They exist, and they have consequences.

#16 The awkward money stuff

Every decision seems so loaded. Do we get appetizers? Dessert? You might think, *I really, really want the salmon, but it's the most expensive item on the menu, and I'm happy to pay for it myself—Jesus, I can afford it—but he probably won't let me pay, so if I order the salmon, is he expecting me to put out? That's out of the question because he has these bushy eyebrows, but damn it, I really do want salmon. Why can't I just pay my fair share? Fine. You win. Pasta.*

#3 There's less room to grow

It's not that dinner is *always* a bad date. It's just a bad first date. When you start with drinks, you can build to restaurants.

#8 The cost

Does avoiding dinner make us cheapskates? Maybe. But it's tough to plunk down a hundred dollars for a woman you don't even really know. Just some truth talk. (Yet are we willing to sleep with a woman we don't really know? Um...no comment.)

To clarify, this doesn't mean that a dinner first date will be a bad first date. Saying you should never do dinner is just as silly as saying you should always do it. I've had plenty of good ones.

Four exceptions where it totally makes sense to have dinner on the first date:

Exception 1:
One of you doesn't drink. If that's the case, dinner can be more comfortable.

Exception 2:
The dude is so loaded that buying a two-hundred-dollar dinner is like buying a pack of gum.

Exception 3:
It's a fun restaurant with gobs of personality—live entertainment, shareable plates, exotic themes, whatever. A lively atmosphere can slice through the formality.

Exception 4 (courtesy of our friend Dave):
"Sometimes it's as simple as 'I'm hungry and I want to eat.' I'm coming from work, I have a second date later, and this is my only chance. So what the hell? We go for a decent meal, I eat most of the food (she's pretending to be dainty), and I spend forty dollars on her."

NEVER TALK ABOUT POLITICS OR RELIGION ON THE FIRST DATE

JEFF

I'm on a first date. It's going well. We just knocked back two rounds of mojitos, we have a good vibe, and she keeps touching my leg.

"So . . . I have some weird . . . political views," she says, flashing a wicked smile.

"Tell me."

"This will offend you." She touches my thigh.

"Impossible," I say.

"You sure?"

I'm sure. I can handle it. Religion, politics, health care, the war in Afghanistan, *bring it.* I'm a talker. I'll talk about anything.

"I think . . . ," she says, still smiling, "that there's a lot of merit to slavery."

Whoa! What! I recoil, flabbergasted, and she quickly clarifies that her kind of slavery would have nothing to do with race or ethnicity—she finds that monstrous—but would instead use intelligence as the deciding factor in whether a person is enslaved or is a slave owner.

We didn't go on a second date.

So part of me is thankful that she broke the "Never talk about politics" rule, as I didn't have to wait until date five, ten, or twenty to discover that she's still fighting the War of Northern Aggression. If you have any political deal breakers—like, say, hot-button issues from the Ulysses S. Grant administration—you might as well discover them early.

But this kind of extreme example is rare, and more often than not, the rule holds a nugget of truth. Let's tweak it to say, "Never talk *too much* about politics or religion on a first date." Politics is like salt. A little bit adds flavor; too much ruins the meal.

When you talk about politics with someone you've just met, you're missing the context that puts what they're saying in perspective. I have plenty of friends across the political spectrum. My own family runs the gamut—Lefties, Righties, Centrists. And it's never an issue, because we already share other interests, a history of friendship, or blood. Take my buddy Gino. He's a lifelong friend. We don't agree on a single political issue, but I'd bail him out of jail, take a bullet for him, and if he ever killed a man, I'd hop on the first flight to Denver and help him bury the body, no questions asked. This is what friends do. But if, when we met in college, the *very first thing* he did was launch into a sixty-minute diatribe on immigration, we never would have had a second man-date.

Some people are blessed with the ability to talk about politics in a way that's friendly, nonpolarizing, and intellectually curious. There are five hundred of these people on this planet. (One of them is Jon Stewart.) If both you and your date are in this special band of five hundred, then yes, chat away. It's possible to talk about issues of *substance* on a first date, and if this bumps elbows with politics now and then, so be it.

The greater risk, however, isn't that you'll offend your date's ideology; the risk is that you'll do something much worse: be boring. When people get riled up about politics, they tend to get preachy and ramble on like a radio talk show host. Enough already, we get it, you hate lobbyists, now can we get another drink, or something even better . . . the check?

I agree with Jeff. And I'd like to add this: don't talk too much about politics, religion, or *anything*, for that matter.

We used to call my friend Katy the "opera singer" because on every date her conversation sounded something like this: "*Me, me, me, me, meeeeeeee!*" Men wanted to date her, but they found the Katy show exhausting.

One of the biggest complaints I hear from both men and women after a first date is that their date talked too much and didn't ask them questions or show much interest in them. In an effort to impress our date, some of us become opera singers, too.

Perhaps it shouldn't be a surprise that people notice when you notice them. In his 1930s bestseller, *How to Win Friends and Influence People*, Dale Carnegie states, "You can make more friends in two months by becoming interested in other people than you can in two years by trying to get other people interested in you."

So at the risk of being verbose while I tell you not to be, let me simply say this: worry less about impressing your date, and let your date impress you. You don't want to create a job interview scenario (in which you're not saying anything and you're running through twenty questions), but you also don't want to recite a monologue about your life, your interests, and your goals while he politely nods his head. One of the sexiest qualities you can have is curiosity.

First Date: Conversation Don'ts

First-date conversations that are worse than politics or religion:

"Yeah." "Maybe." [Silence.] "Okay." [Silence.] "Maybe."
She says nothing, reveals nothing. The opera singer's evil cousin: the mute.
"I've had such *bad luck* in dating!"
Yeah, we all have. Don't go there.
"Oh, so you're on Wall Street. You must be really good at lying."
Feisty flirting is one thing. Challenging the person's core decisions in life is something else. Save that for marriage.

"I should be getting a raise this year, which puts my salary at . . . "

Talking about salaries on a first date is only *slightly* less crude than a guy talking about the size of his, ah, bonus.

"My therapist says that . . . "

This is nothing against therapists—in New York, you're required by city ordinance to have one—but skip this session on the first date.

"So my aunt Mildrew just got her test results back. It's cancer."

Not to sound heartless, but there's a time and a place for talking about the serious life stuff. Yes, you want to be with someone who can talk to you about *real* things, and yes, they should have enough empathy to roll with it, but a date, theoretically, should be an escape from the gloomy side of life. Save this stuff for later.

"My mom is always saying, 'When are you going to get married!'"

Scary. Even as a joke.

"How many times have you read *Gravity's Rainbow*? I've found that you can't really understand it until the fourth read."

Shocking that this person's single, right? It's cool to have an intellectual litmus test, just as long as the execution of said test does not, simultaneously, fail the other person's litmus test for obnoxiousness.

"So I saw on Twitter that it looks like you..."
It's one thing to do an online search; it's another thing to cop to it. Let's all preserve the illusion that we're not cyber-stalkers.

MAKE A PERFECT
FIRST IMPRESSION

ANDREA

I've heard dating advice that encourages people to act perfect when they meet someone new. Apparently, you should look perfectly polished and say all the right things on a first date if you want to land a husband and *a perfect relationship*.

The issue I have with "perfect" is that perfect is an impossible standard for you or anyone to sustain. Perfect is unnatural, inauthentic and, frankly, boring. Perfect may initially impress some, but it makes it difficult for the vast majority of people to connect with you. When we meet people, we're generally looking to find something relatable. We notice the qualities that make people interesting and special, but we also look for the qualities that make them accessible. I'm not interested in being in a relationship with someone who takes herself too seriously—and most people feel the same way.

Consider the people you admire most. Are they perfect? Admitting that you don't know something or showing your quirky

Q: How do I end a date with a guy I'm not interested in seeing again?

ANDREA

A number of men have kissed my ear (not in a sexy way) in an attempt to reach my lips at the end of a first or second date. Awkward.

It's tough to know how to part ways at the end of your date when you know that you don't want to hang out again. Both men and women are guilty of suggesting that they'll keep in touch when they know they don't plan to connect again. Men generally like to avoid uncomfortable moments at every opportunity, so it's not unusual for them to pretend that they'll follow up when they know they won't (Jeff, are you listening? Women hate this!), and women tend not to want to hurt someone's feelings, so they may also pretend there's the potential for more.

So how do you politely exit a date when you know there's no chance of romance? Rather than alluding to any future communication or plans, focus on what you enjoyed about the evening. You can say something like, "Thanks for introducing me to that bar. It was fun. Good to meet you." If your date leans in for a kiss or tries to set up date number two, you can respond with something simple, like, "I don't think we're a romantic match, but I enjoyed meeting you and wish you the best." (Less is more!)

Rejection stings worse the longer it's drawn out. If you're not interested, it's better to send a clear message than to lead someone on, so you can both move on and meet a better match.

(continued)

JEFF

Andrea's right: it's better to have a clean break. And here's another confession: I'm totally guilty of screwing this up.

You know how when you go to the grocery store and the cashier smiles and says, "How's it going?" even if you've eaten a wicked enchilada and now you have food poisoning, you still grit your teeth, clench your stomach, and say something like, "Fine. How 'bout you?"

That's how I approached the end of dates. I thought that even if I wasn't into her, it would be rude—bad manners!—to close the show without a kiss. I'd think, *Okay, well, that was a bad date, but at least we're ending on a proper note.* I know I'm not alone. Many of us, men and women both, feel this compulsive need to just "be nice" at the end of a date. Maybe it's a chaste kiss, maybe it's more, or maybe it's a hollow promise like, "I'll call you soon."

This isn't done out of malice, trickery, or even a desire for first-date sex. (Honest!) The motivation usually involves, well, a compulsive need to avoid awkwardness. I now realize that this is both cruel and self-defeating. It gives the wrong impression, it leads the woman on, and, ironically, it only creates more awkwardness in the future.

It's better to take your lumps and have a bit of weirdness now than lots of weirdness later. A simple hug, a smile, maybe a harmless "Have a good night." Done and done! No one gets misled. And if you don't like the guy, but he tries to kiss you? Don't let him. Give him the cheek, and he'll get the message.

idiosyncrasies is actually attractive, as long as you don't swing too far to the side of being unrelentingly self-deprecating.

In many ways, being authentic is both the easiest—and the hardest—thing you can be. It's tough to expose your true self. (It's much easier to be rejected when putting on a persona.) However, the more you show people what makes you interesting and truly *you*, the more you will make an impression. If the real you doesn't impress him, you can both move on and find a better match. You want someone to like you for who you really are, not some perfect person you're pretending to be.

Put your best foot forward on a date, but know that if you trip a few times, it won't turn a good guy off. In fact, he may even find it endearing.

Why a Guy Loses Interest on a First Date

JEFF

I've been on lots of first dates. If the bank made a First Date Rewards Card that earned you airline miles—Date Dollars?—I'd circle the globe seven times. Most of these first dates didn't go anywhere. Here's why:

There's not a physical connection
Truth talk. Even if I have objective data that says she's the most amazing woman on the planet—like,

say, a think tank from MIT developed a computer algorithm, crunched the numbers, and calculated that she is literally my perfect match—if I lack the red-blooded hunger to kiss her, I'm out. (Reason #238 I'm going to hell.) There are schools of thought that say we grow more attracted to people over time, and that we should give it a chance and let our love blossom. Those schools are probably right, but I've never enrolled. (I promised honesty, not virtue. Also, I hate the word "blossom.")

She can't hide her judgments

I can't remember where, but someone once said, "Judge not, lest ye be judged." That's some lousy advice, right? We all judge. If you can't judge, then you can't make decisions. But it's one thing to internally make judgments—to gather new data, assimilate, reevaluate—and it's another to wear that process on your face. I've been on dates where the woman asked a battery of questions, like "Oh, so you buy nonorganic milk?" True, in some aspects, dating is an audition, but the trick is to hide that scorekeeping.

I don't feel challenged

This doesn't mean we need to argue or bicker. But no one likes a wet blanket.

I can sniff out irreconcilable substantive lifestyle differences

This is more important as you get older. When I was twenty-two, she could be a terrorist who uses heroin, steals from churches, and talks longingly about how good it feels to kill a man. All I'd be thinking was . . . she's so hot. As we age, our priorities change. More realistically, let's say she's a club girl who goes out five nights a week to the trendiest hot spots and always needs to see and be seen. There's nothing wrong with that—I've been there—but it's no longer my wheelhouse.

We're not having fun

"Fun" is an underrated personality trait. We either have it or we don't.

She's not into me

Why does the Dating Advice Industry always frame things as "*He's* not that into you" or "Why won't *he* call?" or "How to get *him* to love your . . ." Isn't that sort of sexist? Dating is a two-way street. For every guy who's not into a girl, there's a girl who's not into a guy. So the reason plenty of my dates didn't work out is that, frankly, she wasn't that into me. And that's okay.

All these reasons have one common thread—they're almost completely gender neutral. They're probably similar to the reasons that you lose interest in a guy. Magazines like to gin up angles, like "What he really thinks on a date!" and "What she really thinks on a date!" I've been guilty of writing these types of articles. (And I'll probably keep doing it. . . . A man's gotta eat.) But we, as humans, are more similar than dissimilar, so when you're trying to decode a guy, it's probably as simple as decoding yourself, and then adding a 10 percent jerk factor.

Chapter 3
MEN YOU SHOULDN'T DATE

The combined forces of pop culture, the status quo, and societal expectations say some very specific things about who you should and shouldn't date. He needs to be this tall, that wealthy, and have a certain kind of job….

- Never date a co-worker
- Date someone age appropriate
- Long-distance relationships don't work
- Men and women can't be friends
- Find a man who makes more money than you

NEVER DATE A CO-WORKER

ANDREA

I remember being one of the first to arrive to math class in seventh grade because I wanted to snag a seat close to my crush, Jonathan. Jonathan was about five inches shorter than me and much better at integers. Learning was more fun with him around.

Fast-forward a decade to my first job out of college. I dressed up in my finest sweater set (hey, it was the 90s!) to impress a new employee a few cubicles over. After a few weeks of our eyeing each other in the hallway, he asked me out and we began a covert office romance that lasted a year. While the relationship started in the office, it did not end because of the office.

As far as I know, our office mates had no idea about the relationship, as we made a conscious decision to separate business and pleasure. And that was part of the excitement! Work is more fun when you have an office crush.

Critics of office romance certainly have a point. If you're more focused on your crush than on your work, you may not meet deadlines for assigned tasks and this will negatively affect your office environment and productivity. And if you're involved with a higher-up, you run the risk of missing out on a promotion, or getting one that others will be cynical of.

For this reason, if you date in the office, it's better to date someone in another department, to keep the relationship quiet for the first few months (until you know it's really going somewhere), and to set ground rules in advance (i.e., if it doesn't work out, you won't launch campaigns against each other at work).

Dating a co-worker is not a "safe" option, but it is an option when you are single and feel a great connection with someone you work with. We have to take risks in dating if we want to find love.

So if you're going to take the risk, be smart about it. Don't date your married boss, and don't share details with every office mate, or the watercooler chatter will heat up fast.

Here are some other strategies for managing office romances:

1. **Don't blab to the whole office** the day after you first hook up. Confide in your friends in the "real world."

2. **Figure out if it's just a fun hookup** or if you see long-term potential with your office crush. If it's just a roll in the hay, it may not be worth taking the risk (and dealing with serious awkwardness); but if it's looking like you may have a future with your office mate, it may be worth exploring.

3. **Finally, if it's explicitly stated in your contract** that office relations are against company policy, ask yourself if it is worth losing your job over your crush. Maybe, but maybe not.

The bottom line is that office romance happens, and I know too many married couples who met at work to dismiss it.

So weigh the risks against the rewards when evaluating the possibility of an office romance. Do a solid cost-benefit analysis. Math crush Jonathan would like that equation.

JEFF

All relationships end poorly: either in a breakup or in death. So given that the odds of doom are approximately 100 percent, why would you risk a lawsuit (very unlikely, but still), risk your job (less unlikely), or risk a post-breakup atmosphere of awkwardness (a near certainty)?

Still, that's like saying, "Always wear your seat belt!" or "Never drink on an empty stomach!" We know it's sound advice, but we tend to break the rule anyway. Thirty-eight percent of the working world has had an office romance, according to CareerBuilder.com's 2011 survey. Sometimes this works out and they'll get married, they'll buy homes in Connecticut, and they'll share cute baby photos on Tumblr. In fact, that same survey found that 31 percent of office romances lead to marriage. (Just to clarify, they'll still die. I'm not completely wrong, you know.)

But if you're going to do it? Do it right. I endorse Andrea's guidelines, and I'll throw out these, as well:

Don't do it just for a fling

Too much risk, too little upside. It's one thing to
date someone at work because there's real potential
for a serious relationship, but why risk your career for
a bit of booty? There are better and safer places to find
casual sex, such as jail and church.

Don't be office shmooopy shmoopies

This rule is less about saving your job, and more about
saving your co-workers the need to purchase razors and
slit their wrists.

Go offline

Avoid company email, company Instant Messaging,
company BBMs. You know all the messy lawsuits that hinge
on email printouts? Those couples started out happy, too.

Date outside your solid line

"Solid line" as in a solid line on the org chart. It's
one thing to date a dude who sits on the other side of
the building—maybe you never officially work with
him, say—and it's something else to date your boss or
employee. Relationships are tricky as it is. Jobs are tricky
as it is. But if you're the literal boss of your boyfriend?
Love + Work is not like combining chocolate and
peanut butter. It's like combining chocolate and shit.

Know that you are less subtle than you think

We all think we're super sneaky. But it's pretty easy to get
exposed—a lingering glance, a hand on the shoulder.

Be even more cautious than you think is necessary. That said, at some point, you also need to do the following:

Come out of the closet

Eventually go public, or else you'll never really know if the relationship is real or if it's just propped up by the thrill of naughtiness.

Leave the work-talk at work

The hidden downside of a work relationship. If you're not careful, you could find that deadlines, office politics, and the drudgery of work will ooze into your dinners and picnics and even into your bedroom. If I've learned one thing in life, it's this: there's no worse foreplay than a talk about the 3rd Quarter Budget.

Always treat each other with respect

The stakes are just too high. Look, no matter how you slice it, there's a decent chance that your romance will end in a breakup. (Remember the earlier stat? Thirty-one percent of romances lead to marriage... but that means that 69 percent end in tears.) So it's crucial that you treat each other with respect during the relationship, during the breakup and, most important, even after the breakup.

DATE SOMEONE AGE APPROPRIATE

Lurking beneath the concept of "age appropriateness"—which seems sensible enough—are two sub-rules that Andrea and I hear a lot, rules that foment anxiety and fear:

1. Men aren't interested in women over thirty.
2. If he's over thirty and single, something's wrong with him.

Any truth to these?

Men aren't interested in women over thirty

Here's what men are interested in: attractive women. Attractive women come in many different shapes and sizes. They can be younger. They can be older. They can be white or black or blonde or brunette. But what matters is that we find them *attractive*. This is backed up by science, as neurological studies have shown that men's brains are more responsive to visual stimuli. Also backed up by science: we're dicks.

(Quick tangent: By saying "what really matters is that they're attractive," we're now in the Brutal Honesty Zone, and

I'm not suggesting that physical attractiveness is the only thing that matters, or that it's the most important ingredient. It's not. A woman's personality, intelligence, charm, sense of humor, integrity, and appreciation for the mid-90s Houston Rockets—that's what counts in the long run. But when you first meet someone? For 99 percent of men—and, I'd suspect, a large percentage of women—looks are the "first filter." If you don't want to make out with them, a winning personality is a moot point.)

Back to the age question. For most men, we think in terms of "She's hot" or "She's busted." We don't think in terms of "She's hot, but unfortunately, she's 35" or "She's busted, but she's only 22!" True, many men are skittish about dating women older than them, and the precise reasons for this are understood by no one. But the question pivots on her age *relative to the man* (is she older than me?), not on whether she's over 30 or over 40. Are there dating ageists? Sure. Just as there are dating racists. It's ugly, unfair, unfortunate. But just like with racism, ageism says more about the man than it does the woman.

A 37-year-old guy who will only date early-20-some-things . . . red flag. He's probably immature, he's probably still looking for flings, or maybe he has some control fetish, perceiving younger women as less of a challenge. If the 37-year-old guy is ready for an *actual relationship*, he probably won't care if she's 35. And if he does? There's something wrong with him.

Speaking of . . .

If he's over 30 and single, something's wrong with him

True or false?

True. There's something wrong with all of us. But in a larger sense?

Yawn. This rule was undoubtedly useful in the days of Jane Austen novels. Back then we got married by 19, bought a house by 23, and spawned three teenage daughters before we hit 40.

Since then a miraculous thing has happened: *we've lived our lives.* We found that, shockingly, it's okay to have multiple relationships in our 20s (as opposed to marrying our high school sweetheart) and that it's okay to focus on our careers, and we found that if we haven't yet met The One, there's no rush to crank out a family and settle for Not The One. Some people call this "having issues." I call this progress.

Note: Am I at all biased, and am I stating all of the above because I, too, am now in my midthirties and still single? No, not at all, not defensive or protective at all!

Whenever I've set people up to date, the first three questions they generally ask are, "What does he/she look like?" "What does he/she do?" "How old is he/she?" (Interestingly, we tend to collect superficial data when trying to determine if someone may be compatible with us. I've rarely heard someone ask,

"What kind of values does he/she have?" or "Is she/he close with the family?")

The odds are that most of us will end up married to someone who's around our age. According to a 2009 U.S. census report, the national average age at which men and women marry for the first time is 28.3 years old for men and 26.5 for women. (These numbers look different in different parts of the country. People marry much later in New York City and San Francisco than they do in Utah, for instance, but the age gap between men and women remains consistent, at about two years.)

In a 2012 *New York Post* article, two single writers reflected on their disillusionment with dating men of a certain age in Manhattan. They state, "I wonder if fans [of *Sex and the City*] know that rent-controlled apartments like Carrie's are as hard to come by as a good-looking, well-adjusted single guy over the age of 35."

The writers' assessment isn't uncommon. How many times have you heard (or perhaps said), "I would* never date a man who is 35 or 40 years old and still single! Something must be wrong with him"? I hear it all the time.

Ironically, a number of women who propose the theory that a guy must be damaged goods if he's over 35 and single are themselves over 35 and single. These same women tend to bemoan

---

* As I mentioned earlier, I'm not a fan of the words *never* and *can't* in dating (or in life, for that matter). How can one know about the "nevers" in one's life before one has experienced them?

the fact that men their age aren't interested in them and only want to date women in their 20s.

Age biases exist in dating for both men and women. Just as some women complain that a guy over 35 must have issues, there are men in their 30s and 40s who say that single women their age have too much "baggage" and are therefore undateable. Some of these men worry that women over 30 will rush (even trick!) them into marriage and parenthood before they're ready.

Assigning characteristics to people we don't know is generally a bad approach when forming relationships. I know as many neurotic and needy 22-year-olds as I do 38-year-olds. I've met incredibly grounded women who are a decade younger than I am, and I'm constantly reminded that just because someone looks like an adult, it doesn't mean she acts like one.

Age is not irrelevant, of course, but it's not a sufficient criterion on its own to give you an accurate picture of someone's readiness for the relationship he or she is looking for. Chances are someone who is older has a little more experience, which will be threatening to some and refreshing for others.

Rather than deciding that a 35- or a 40-year-old never married man must have "issues" (don't we all?), consider another perspective. Maybe like you, or someone great that you know who is of a certain age and is single, he has dedicated time to pursuing a career or had a long-term relationship that didn't work out. Or maybe he *is* a freak. But you won't learn that from his age alone.

The questions you should ask yourself when evaluating a potential relationship are, "Are we both in a similar chapter of our life in terms of our needs and wants? Do we share similar values?"

Judge each person individually, and challenge your beliefs about men of a certain age. After all, wouldn't you want to be given the same chance?

LONG-DISTANCE RELATIONSHIPS DON'T WORK

ANDREA

In 1999 I met a great guy at a concert while visiting a friend in California. He and I clicked immediately. (I even joked that we were Y2K compatible. Ouch.) Since I hadn't met too many people like him in my hometown, I felt that it was worth getting to know him better. I was living in Toronto at the time and was in grad school, and the decision to stay in touch with him was not very practical...but since when is following your heart practical?

I went back to Canada shortly after we met, and we both knew that we'd keep in touch. Over the next few months, he and I exchanged countless emails and phone calls and spent many hours (and too much money) flying back and forth, getting to know each other better. Some people told me I was crazy—since long-distance relationships never work out—but I was determined to see how compatible we really were.

Life challenges came up while we navigated our relationship across the continent. Over our year of being together apart, his grandfather died, and I felt overwhelmed with all the questions that inevitably pop up when school ends. During these times, he and I leaned on each other for support. Of course, we didn't physically comfort each other, but that didn't mean that we weren't connected in a deep and intimate way. We depended on each other the way that any couple in a committed relationship would.

After twelve months of great (and sometimes difficult and exhausting) cross-country visits and lengthy conversations, I moved across the country to live with my boyfriend in San Francisco. We lived there together for five years.

My relationship with my long-distance love didn't work out, but it had nothing to do with the way in which it started. It was one of my most significant relationships, and he's one of my closest friends today.

We've all heard tales of people who got burned by trying to date someone who lived far away from them, and warnings for those considering it. Popular theories about why long-distance relationships don't work point to the fact that you can't fairly gauge your compatibility when you're always sharing heightened, wonderful moments, instead of experiencing "real life" with another person.

I understand that perspective. After all, it's easy to get along with someone when times are good. The true test of a person's character and your compatibility as a couple is seeing how your partner responds to a bad day or how you react to a challenge together. My friend Natalie's grandmother gave her the wise advice to "weather a man through all the seasons" before deciding to be with him.

But just because you don't live in the same area code doesn't mean you don't see each other through the proverbial ups and downs of life. If you're in a committed relationship, you can pretend that your life is picture-perfect for only so long....

The rule "Long-distance relationships don't work" simply doesn't hold water, since we all know couples who started out this way. So perhaps a better rule is "Long-distance relationships don't work without the necessary work to make them work." (I realize that doesn't necessarily roll off the tongue.)

This relationship is an investment, but if you really see potential with another person, it's perhaps the best investment you will ever make.

Don't rule someone out just because he's in another area code, but keep these steps in mind:

Regular visits
Long-distance relationships won't work if you don't keep up the momentum by seeing each other regularly—as much as your schedule and your bank

account can handle. Every time you leave your long-distance lover, you should have another date on the books to keep up the momentum.

Get out

Long-distance couples have a tendency to spend many hours cooped up together when they reunite after many days or weeks away, but it's just as important to see your partner in his world—with his friends, his family, his interests—so you can make an informed decision about your compatibility.

Be present

My friend Brian* used to have a habit of making every plan last minute, but when he was in a long-distance relationship with Jill, he couldn't be as spontaneous. Long-distance relationships can turn even the most "Carpe diem!" person into a future-obsessed planner. Since there are no guarantees about your future (in any relationship!), try to stay present during your time together.

Think ahead

Sounds like I'm contradicting myself, no? As much as you should stay present, it's equally important to find time to discuss where things may be headed. Such questions are natural in any adult relationship, so don't be scared of them when they pop up. It's important to

---

* Brian and Jill married in 2007, moved to her hometown of Toronto, and have two kids now. Awww.

figure out how realistic it would be for one of you to move eventually. If neither of you would ever relocate, the long-distance factor may be a deal breaker.

Clearly they can, as we all know friends who survived the Long D. And according to some data from the Center for the Study of Long Distance Relationships (yes, that actually exists), the breakup percentages for normal relationships and long-distance ones are roughly even, with long-distance actually coming out the winner:

	Normal	Long Distance
Breakup % in first month	30%	27%
Breakup % in first 3 months	21%	37%
Breakup % in first 6 months	35%	42%
Breakup % in first year	25%	8%

True, these stats have a self-selection bias, as you have to really, really, really like someone before you even try long distance. But the point is…these relationships *can* work. The more interesting question is, *what* makes them work?

You need six ingredients. It's what I call the L.D. DATE. (Confession: I've never actually called it that.)

Lots of visits
Easier to pull off when you're a little older and have a little more cash. If you can see the dude for two long weekends a month, you're doing better than most short-distance relationships.

Daily communication . . . without saturation
Yes, it's cliché (if true) to say, "You must communicate!" but make sure these conversations don't turn into the daily Big Phoners where you parse the nuance of your breakfast cereal.

Doing laundry time
Most people think that "missing the person" is the most challenging aspect of a long-distance relationship. That's the most obvious one, but there's actually a sneakier, more fundamental challenge: the lack of Doing Laundry Time. When you're in the Long D, it's easy to slip into the cycle of Amazing Weekend > 3 Weeks of Longing > Amazing Weekend > 3 Weeks of Longing > ad infinitum. In this pattern, you run the risk of being so absorbed in missing the person—and then so happy to see them on the weekend—that you never face the real, brass-tacks issues that other couples deal with all the time, questions like "Who's friends do we hang out with tonight?" or "Why are you so messy around the house?" In other words, what are you guys *really like* when you're your natural selves, just doing laundry together?

A normal relationship before the long-distance relationship

This isn't a hard requirement, but your odds are higher if you don't *start* the relationship in the Long D. If you've already been with the guy for a year and then you spend six months apart? Different story from meeting the dude in Vegas, hooking up, and then becoming boyfriend/girlfriend while you're in Dallas and he's in Buenos Aires.

Trust

Needs to be rock solid. Proved by science: if you think there's a greater than 5 percent chance that he will cheat or you will cheat, there's a 95 percent chance that the long-distance relationship will fail.

And finally, it's best to have an . . .

End point

An open-ended long-distance relationship is like an open-ended war. It might be popular in the short term, but eventually you'll need to bring the troops home.

MEN AND WOMEN CAN'T BE FRIENDS

We almost didn't cover this rule, as it's not, technically, a rule about *who you should date*. But it's such an iconic rule that it demands inclusion....

JEFF

This should be simple, right? As platonic friends, a man and woman should be able to watch a movie, eat ice cream, or go to the dog park together without, necessarily, ending up naked. Isn't the ability to control our impulses, to master our id, what separates humans from other species? That, and thumbs?

It's baffling. We can do so much as a species. We've cured polio, created democracy, invented spray-on sunscreen. But it's true. More often than not, Billy Crystal was right: men and women can't be friends if one of them wants to have sex with the other.

Unless you meet any of the following exceptions:

Exception 1: One of you is married.
AND
The married person's partner is super-cool/trusting/ awesome
AND
The man and the woman are extraordinarily respectful about appropriateness.
AND
You both know in your deepest heart of hearts that you would never, ever cross any lines. And even then, even

in this rare circumstance, it's still kinda weird for the two of you to always hang out together. When someone's married, there's a different word for BFF—spouse.

Exception 2: If you both just know that you're not a romantic fit, and you both know that if you hook up, you would ruin the friendship, so you never go there.

This could work. Careful, though. It's easy to be out of sync. The woman could think they're a "bad romantic fit," while the man is still hopelessly in love Gabriel García-Márquez-style.

Exception 3: If he's "grandfathered in."

Maybe he's been a childhood friend of yours since you played Legos, and you think of him as a brother. This works in a vacuum. But will your new boyfriend also think of him as a brother? It gets tricky. Sure, it can still work, but it usually involves throttling down the original friendship, even if that friendship always is, always has been, and always will be G-rated.

Exception 4: If you hooked up long ago and slackened the tension.

Halley's Comet. Happens once every seventy-six years. You're good enough friends that you can look past a little romantic hiccup . . . and you never speak of it again, or if you do, you laugh about it. (See *Seinfeld*'s Jerry and Elaine.)

Exception 5: If a new guy meets you in a bookstore, asks for your number, and says he wants to hang out, as friends.

Ha! That's a trick. This is in no way platonic. If he's straight and single and you're single, *the guy wants to sleep with you.* Always. In fact, pretty much every guy wants to sleep with you. It's true! When the "new friend from your spinning class" or the "nice guy on the train who helped you carry your IKEA bags" says that you should get drinks sometime, this is not a friendly overture. It boggles my mind how many intelligent, attractive, otherwise world-savvy women seem to misread men's intentions and give us the "friendly" benefit of the doubt. Don't give us the benefit of the doubt. We never deserve the benefit of the doubt.

One last thought. The English language doesn't even have a word for this kind of relationship. Consider: as a woman, you could say, "I'm headed to the beach with my girlfriends," and it's understood that you mean your platonic girlfriends, who you are not screwing. But you can't say, "I'm headed to the beach with my boyfriends" without sounding like a polygamist.

ANDREA

It's normal for the lines to be blurry in a male/female friendship when you're both single and straight, but that doesn't mean you will (or shouldn't) cross the friendship line.

In college I was close friends with a guy named Chuck. (That's not true. His name wasn't really Chuck, but out of respect to this man, I've decided to change his name.) Chuck and I did everything together. He was the guy I went to when I needed a study buddy or a movie date. He and I would stay up late talking about everything and would knock on each other's dorm rooms in the morning to make sure the other didn't oversleep. If two days went by without hanging out with Chuck, I noticed his absence and missed him.

Secretly, I knew Chuck liked me as more than just a friend, though if you asked my 20-year-old self, I'd swear to you that he saw me in the platonic way I saw him. Chuck was wonderful, but I wasn't drawn to him romantically. He was big and cuddly like a Bernese mountain dog. I didn't tell him that.

Chuck and I hung out every day for months, until one night I cried on his shoulder because I felt insecure and ugly. (Did I mention I was a really needy 20-something-year-old?) I should note that Jack Daniel's was in the room with me that night, as well, so maybe I wouldn't have been so slobbery and pathetic if I'd been sober. Chuck was a little intoxicated himself and consoled me in a sloppy yet assertive way. He told me I was beautiful ("I am?"), that I was special ("Really?"), and that anyone who didn't think so was crazy. He mentioned that I had the nicest smile he had ever seen, and he wanted me to stop crying so he could see it again. A moment later, I gazed into Chuck's eyes and we shared our first kiss. It was passionate and sweet at the same time. I fell asleep in his arms later that night.

The next morning I woke up to the sound of applause in Chuck's living room. I soon discovered his three roommates were actually sharing high fives with him for "going for it." I realized, of course, that I was "it," and "it" was something Chuck had been speaking to them about for a while. As I tried to find my bra in Chuck's bed, my mind was racing. *Is my friendship with Chuck real? Has he just been trying to get me in bed since we met?* I was confused. These thoughts flooded in, especially since I had a sobering wake-up call that morning—even after our passionate night, I still didn't see Chuck as a romantic match.

Over the next few weeks of awkwardly trying to transition our friendship to a relationship, I made the very mature move of going MIA and ignoring all Chuck's calls and attempts to get together. Our friendship never recovered.

I'm not sure that men and women can't be friends, but I am sure that when a friend is as disrespectful as I was at that time, it's hard to salvage the relationship.

I've heard many theories about whether or not men and women can be friends. In the iconic "men and women can't be friends" movie, *When Harry Met Sally*, Harry echoes the very common belief that it's not realistic to have a friendship with the opposite sex "because the sex part always gets in the way."

Since my friendship with Chuck ended many years ago, I've had platonic male friends (this time I'm sure), and I actually married a guy who was once kept in the friend zone because he wasn't my type. I lost some male friends when I got married or when they got hitched, and just like with my female friendships, some of my male relationships have shifted over time.

What I'm sure of is this: the guys who I ruined a friendship with because we crossed the romance line were never really in the relationship in the first place to be my buddy. The guys that I'm currently friends with are appealing and interesting (or I wouldn't be friends with them!), but I don't feel that they're scheming to get in my underpants, and I quite enjoy having them in my life. It's amazing to have a male perspective, in addition to the one I hear from my husband, Michael, and my gay best friend, Steve.

It's not unusual for question marks or gray zones to exist in some male/female relationships. You and your friend were drawn to each other because you liked something about each other, after all. Most of us seek out relationships and friendships with people we are attracted to. Of course, the attraction doesn't always have to be sexual, but the odds are higher that a man and a woman who are both cute, single, and straight will wonder if the relationship could be more.

If you think you may have something solid with a male friend that could possibly lead to a happy romance and you sense he has the same feelings, not only do I think it's okay to explore a romantic relationship, but I would also encourage it. Relationships require taking risks and putting yourself out there. Whether it's with a good male friend or an online date, you'll never be able to predict the outcome of a new romantic relationship without testing the waters.

Don't let the fact that you're friends with someone great get in the way of the potential to share a romantic relationship with him. Friendship is a necessary factor in our long-term relationships. If anything, you should be more worried about the guys you date who you would never want to be friends with or who possess qualities that you would never tolerate in your other relationships.

FIND A MAN WHO MAKES MORE MONEY THAN YOU

ANDREA

One of the greatest things that happened to my career was marrying a teacher who didn't earn a lot of money.

In the past, I dated men who made a very good living, including a couple of CEOs, who wined and dined me, purchased pricey gifts for me, and assured me that I could continue pursuing my goals to write, teach workshops, and coach without worrying about money.

Even though I don't care much about fancy jewelry or designer shoes, I'm a glutton for interesting experiences. Some of those experiences are free (in fact, I believe the best ones are), but some experiences, like traveling or seeing Broadway shows, add up. It was nice to know that I could maintain a good quality of life. There was just one problem with my approach: I was relying on a man to provide these opportunities for me.

This may offend you as a strong, independent woman, but it wasn't conscious on my part. I have always been highly motivated and independent and have prided myself on paying my own bills, but somewhere deep inside of me, I was sure I'd be financially set because I'd marry one of these great guys with a "good job." I know a number of women who feel that way, too, and who put certain men in the "don't date" category because of their financial position.

When I first started dating my friend Michael, a public school teacher, I had to think differently about how I'd be able to have the kind of life I wanted. At first I thought, *I'll just have to give up some of the things I enjoy doing...*, but then I realized that I could actually have what I wanted if I worked harder. Shocking, right? I don't know why it never occurred to me before.

I'm not motivated solely by money (being a writer would be a bad move, if so), but being with someone who earned a modest salary was a catalyst for my success. Once I started getting more serious with Michael, who believed in me and brought out my best, my career started to grow. I networked to find opportunities, and I started to generate my own work. I realized that if I couldn't find a job I liked, I'd have to create one. I put myself through the coaching program on credit, knowing that one day I'd be successful enough to pay it off. For the first time, I believed that I could attain the comfortable life that I'd been waiting for a man to provide for me.

I followed my heart in my relationship and in my career. Those things go hand in hand, by the way. Somehow when I was confused about men in the past, I didn't have the same space in my head (or heart) to work so creatively.

Every year as my relationship grows, my career expands. There's still a long way for me to go, of course, but had I relied on one of these other successful men, I know that I wouldn't have challenged myself as much as I have, and I don't believe I'd be living my passion today. There's certainly something to the expression "Necessity is the mother of invention."

So this is why I say that marrying a teacher was one of the greatest career moves for me. (I still think teachers should be paid more, but that's a different book.)

Back to you. Is a guy's earning power a deal breaker? Do you favor a guy who makes six figures over one who is home by six? (These things aren't always mutually exclusive, but often they are.) You may not know the answers yet, and you have every right to want what you want. But in today's society, where women are graduating in larger numbers than men and where single, childless women are outearning men in their 20s, it seems that the "Man should make more money than you" rule is old news. Besides, a guy can outearn you with his "good job" and lose it. (Just think of all those wealthy men we knew before the market crashed in 2008.)

Rather than focusing on finding a guy with a good job, focus on what's important about that. Do you like a man who is smart and driven? Focus on that. Be open to the fact that a "driven" guy may show up with a different job or in a different package than you expect. When you don't rely on a man to provide your ideal lifestyle, you may show up differently, too....

JEFF

Welcome to 1957! Ah, the good 'ol days. When a woman's only job was to make sure the meatloaf was ready by 7 p.m., when we didn't have to worry about nonsense like "equal rights," when you could puff cigarettes when you're pregnant, and when the man's supposed to make more money than the woman.

Can we finally put this rule to bed? I'd like to think we've evolved, and thankfully, the stats are now backing this up. As Liza Mundy reports in *The Richer Sex: How the New Majority of Female Breadwinners Is Transforming Sex, Love, and Family,* according to the 2009 Bureau of Labor Statistics, "almost 40 percent of U.S. working wives now outearn their husbands."

It gets better. In large cities single women in their 20s earn on average 8 percent more than single men, according to the 2008 census. We've always known that women are as smart, competent, and ambitious as men. That's not news. But the economics are finally starting to catch up, so it's time we ditch this ridiculous rule.

This doesn't mean that money is irrelevant. And it doesn't mean that you should feel guilty for wanting a guy who's ambitious, fiscally responsible, and can make a good living. And there are some legitimate issues—if the woman is the breadwinner, what happens when she gets pregnant? Is he okay with being Mr. Mom? Those questions are all fair game, and a girl's gotta have standards. But the standard should be pegged to some objective baseline—i.e., "the man is responsible," "the man isn't a mooch." The standard shouldn't be "he makes more money than me."

See also the case of the Lawyer and the Circle Painter, pages 6–7.

Q: Why do guys act like douches?

JEFF

I'll start with my own story, and then we'll see what we can extrapolate.

Growing up, I was a big dork who never talked to girls. Why didn't girls like me? I can think of only 1,378 reasons. Here are a few:

I didn't just *play* Dungeons & Dragons. I lived it. We didn't wear robes or tunics, thank the elves, but in junior high we did the next best thing: we formed a neighborhood knighthood, complete with Squires and Pages. We used broomsticks, duct tape, and pillows to forge weapons—these became our maces, knives, and scimitars. We staged fencing competitions in the front yard. Publicly. Around this time my parents divorced, and I promised myself I would never get married. There's no better way to keep that promise than never to date anyone, right?

I played on our high school's first lacrosse team. This was Texas, football country, so the entire concept of "lacrosse" seemed alien and effete. On a legendarily bad team, I was the worst player, sniffing the field only because we lacked enough volunteers. Most of our coach's time, I think, was spent designing plays that would keep me as far from the action as possible.

I was the president of our school's debate team, which meant that I was also president of the Celibacy Club. I didn't have a girlfriend until I was 21. I wore a calculator watch.

How is this all relevant? The full story takes another sixty thousand words, but in a nutshell, things began to look up when I joined

(continued)

the Marine Corps Reserve, got in shape, swapped my glasses for contacts, and started to shed the awkwardness. In my early 20s, I flipped a switch. Suddenly I could talk to girls. Suddenly I could go on dates. Suddenly I could vanquish all these demons from my dorky childhood. Things snowballed. When I found out that I *could* date, I wanted to date all the time, and I wanted to date her, and her, and her, and maybe her.

I got a high from going to bars and getting numbers. Every new digit was one more "F" you" to my virginal past. I wasn't dating authentically. I never *lied* about my intentions, per se, but I wasn't looking to meet a girl, see how things go, and then, if we both liked each other, maybe ease into something more serious. I was serial dating with an agenda, even if I kept that agenda from myself.

I treated dating like a game, a sport. My friends and I scoped out bars for the "optimal targets," hatched strategies, and, yes, created our rules. (Example: "He who hesitates is lost," meaning that, in a bar, you need to approach the woman as soon as possible. We had no way of knowing that this would also be one of the rules in Neil Strauss's *The Game*.) My friends outgrew this; I didn't. I never *meant* to be a jerk, I never meant to hurt anyone, and I felt pangs of guilt after every doomed encounter. But this was my cycle of behavior. Get digits, maybe call, maybe go on a few dates, maybe hook up, but never anything serious.

At the time, I comforted myself by saying, "It's okay, you're not leading these women on, you're not promising anything, you're both just having fun." That's what I told myself. In hindsight? *Not promising anything* isn't enough. Dating—or at least adult dating—has an implied understanding that if things go well, maybe there's something down the road. It doesn't have to be marriage, but there should at least be the *possibility* of a three-month relationship, right? For me, that possibility didn't exist.

The roots of all of this, of course, were my irrational needs to prove myself, to overcompensate, to keep slaying those demons . . . long after they were dead. And the root of *this*, of course, was insecurity. This wasn't something I could fix overnight, and it wasn't something that could be fixed by the "right girl" or a girl who could "change me."

Every guy has a different story. Every guy has a different complex. So while I can't claim to speak for the entire Y chromosome, I'm willing to bet that this same root cause—insecurity, coupled by a fear of commitment—has a lot to do with douchebaggery. Maybe the guy isn't mean-spirited, maybe the guy's not a jerk in the other facets of his life, but when it comes to how he approaches women, if you think he's damaged goods? Walk away.*

---

* Over brunch I was chatting with my friend Amy about dating. She looked me in the eyes, hard, and said, "Jeff, you know, not *all* men are assholes. And if you pretend they are, you're letting women off the hook. You're making us seem like victims."

It's a fair point. So let me clarify to Amy and the world. At heart, no, I don't believe that all men are jerks or that most men are jerks (except the guys who wear deep V-necks and sunglasses at night—total ass-hats). When things don't work out romantically, it's not simply—or necessarily—because "the guy's a douche." Nine times out of ten, when things go south, it's due to either a lack of chemistry, an attraction imbalance, or because the woman cheated with Robert Pattinson. No one's blameless. No one's off the hook.

Chapter 4
DIGITAL DATING

The conventional wisdom simply hasn't caught up. Thanks to the warp speed of the internet, the rules of 2007 are no longer relevant, much less the rules of 1997.

- Online dating is only for losers
- Never friend a crush on Facebook
- If he's into you, he'll call (not text)
- Always unfriend an ex

ONLINE DATING IS ONLY FOR LOSERS

The millions of people who use online dating sites can't be wrong. (Well, that's not necessarily true. Millions of people can be wrong. See: pre–Copernicus astronomy, the use of LOL, and *Two and a Half Men*. But you know what I mean.)

When confronted, many of the holdouts will *claim* that they think online dating is okay, but will then refuse to try it themselves, thinking that they "don't need it." This is a polite way of saying, "Ha! You want me to do online dating? I can get a date. I go on dates. I'm not a loser."

And while it's true that no one "needs" online dating, it does have certain merits. People who make good boyfriends/girlfriends do not necessarily make good meet-at-the-bar-ers. You have that one friend who's good-looking, funny, and has less game than Steve Carell in *The 40-Year-Old Virgin*. With online dating he can slice through the meet-and-greet phase, skipping to the part that he's good at—the relationship itself—which, in the end, is all that counts. It also lets you filter out the deal breakers. How many times have you liked a guy, only to find out on Date Six that he's a Scientologist?

Until I tried it, online dating just seemed like a chore. I thought it had all the drudgery of a job search, demanding a résumé (dating profile page), a cover letter (flirty email), a screening interview (phone call), and thank-you notes (second flirty email). Who has time for all that? But there's a way to avoid this paper chase. I included this at the bottom of my profile page: "I'm a little old-fashioned in that I'd prefer to go from online to offline sooner rather than later. The world's greatest cyber-courtship won't—can't—offset a lack of chemistry. If we're both interested, let's meet."

Women seemed to appreciate that, they said they felt the same way, and this helped avoid tedious rounds of back-and-forth emails that leech the joy out of courtship.

Online dating doesn't mean you've given up on "normal" dating. You can do both. And the very term *online dating* is a misnomer, as the dates themselves are offline. It's more like "Online Opportunity to Meet People You Might Want to Offline Date," or OOMPY-M-WOD, for short.

> ### Five things I've learned from
> ### OOMPY-M-WOD

I had a torrid affair with OkCupid. It started as an assignment for *Glamour*—this let me do it without shame—and it quickly became addictive. The shame is gone, the dates were real, and I met some amazing women. Five lessons learned:

1. Brevity counts.

A few women sent me long, loooooonnnng messages as introductions. This was flattering...and oddly frustrating. It made replying seem like work.

2. **Quirks trump perks.**

   I don't really want to hear about the elite perks she
   gets, thanks to her awesome high-powered job. That
   sounds like she's brandishing her résumé. Instead
   I want the quirks.

3. **If her only photo is a head shot, I'll probably pass.**
   Reason #489 I'm going to hell. Look, I don't expect
   her to have some supermodely body—I sure as
   hell don't have one—but if I see only her face, then
   I assume she has something to hide.

4. **Cyber-rejections are frequent and (eventually)
   painless.**

   The best thing about online dating: the upside is
   high and the downside is low. I've messaged plenty
   of women without a response. Who cares? You
   can't fall in love (or even lust) from a profile page.
   There's no damage. And I have to think this is
   gender neutral, so if you message some guy and
   he never pings you back, so what, right? His loss.

Wait, but is it okay for you to message the guy first? What would
"the rules" say? On that note . . .

5. **I won't think any less of her for messaging me first.**
   On some of my best online dates, the woman reached
   out to me first. It's not a turnoff.

> Q: Are Facebook and other social media sites a good way to meet dates?

JEFF

There's a word for people who troll around Facebook and other such sites, reach out to people they don't know, and spark a casual conversation in the hopes that, in the future, it will lead to something sexual: *pedophiles*.

Kidding, kidding, kidding. (Mostly.) To clarify, everything I say here does not apply to dating sites like Match. Those sites are intended for romance—fair game. But when a dude you've never met Friend Requests you on Facebook, comments on your status updates, and then "likes" your bikini photos from 2010? Creepy. Instead of cyber-stalking, maybe we could all do something kinda crazy and, I don't know, meet people at a bar?

But here's the good news! When a strange guy reaches out to a woman on Facebook, unless he's really, really good-looking,

ANDREA

I'm willing to bet that you know someone who found a great relationship through an online dating site. In fact, you probably know a number of people who found love this way. These days online dating is not only a viable way to find a partner, but it's one of the most popular. Over forty million Americans, close to half of the single he will look skeezy. Yet this does not work both ways. Men have less pride. If a hot woman sends us a Friend Request, this is our process:

1. Stare at every photo for an embarrassingly long time.
2. Find out if she's a spambot.
3. If she's not a spambot...stare at her photos some more.
4. If she's a spambot...stare at her photos some more.

We're okay with it! So there you have it. Ninety-nine percent of gender inequities are stacked against women. The burden of pregnancy, discrimination, double-standards, and heels. This is one thing—maybe the only thing!—that puts men at a disadvantage. Enjoy this privilege and live it up.

population, subscribe to dating sites. In 2010 one in five people who married credited an online dating service for the introduction.

Gone are the days when people who made a connection online have to make up a story that their friend "errr...Jay" (as in JDate) set them up, or have to pretend that they met their significant other in the "real world." Here's the thing: online dating *is* the real world. If you're single and looking and not looking online, you're missing out.

For those of you who haven't tapped the World Wide Web for love, the key is to remember that while it's one fantastic way to get dates, it's certainly not the only way. Don't have an all-or-nothing mentality about online dating, or you'll burn out fast. Online dating can be exhausting because of the seemingly endless array of options, the emails, the exchanges, the weird dates, and the disappointments.

Expect to meet freak-show Bob when you venture into cyberspace. As my friend Janna said after meeting the love of her life online, "I'm lucky to have met my husband, Mike, on eHarmony. It was between him and a toothless man from Saskatoon...."

Online dating is like the popular discount department store T.J.Maxx. You'll have to sift through some junk and have patience to find the gems, but finding those gems, whether they turn into a romantic relationship, a friendship, or a new business contact, makes the whole experience worthwhile. And there are plenty of wonderful catches online. With so many millions using online dating, you're bound to find a little of everything.

Keep in mind that in online dating, you have a very small window to make an impression. A good photo and a snappy essay may be the difference between someone clicking on you or clicking away.

Photos

You in Cabo last year with girlfriends, you with your 3-year-old nephew, you close up, you looking back, you...you...you. It's too much. Research shows that too many photos in an online profile is overwhelming to the viewer, who starts to wonder what you *really* look like.

Choose two to three photos of yourself. Ideally, one should be close enough that the viewer can see your face and one should be a full-length shot. (Like it or not, the average online dater reports that if someone doesn't show her body, he assumes she's hiding something.)

And make the photos recent! You want your date to recognize you when you meet in person.

Essay

The "essay" that online dating sites ask you to write is not meant to be taken literally. It's amazing to see how many people contribute a small thesis on the merits of dating them or on what they're looking for in their lives. Their essays may be thoughtful and intelligent, but consider online dating like speed dating. The average viewer makes an immediate judgment call based on very little criteria. Keep your "About Me" concise and upbeat. You'd be surprised how many people lead with negativity: "I think online dating is stupid, but I promised my mom I'd try it...." Great! You seem like a fun person to hang out with!

It's equally hard to stand out if you declare something generic, like, "I have a wonderful life and am looking to share it with a special someone" or "I work hard and play hard." If you want to mention something about your wonderful life, share *why* that's the case. Specifics are a great way to capture someone's interest and also make it easier for someone to contact you. Rather than saying, "I love to travel," invite dialogue with something like, "I loved climbing Machu Picchu. Any ideas on the next mountain I should climb?" or "I believe pizza should be a food group. What's the best slice in the city?" Finally, *show. Don't tell.* Being funny is a much better approach than telling your audience, "I'm told I'm hilarious!"

One more note about online dating. It wasn't invented for us to have e-relationships. Communicate three to six times and then book the date if you're still intrigued. Otherwise everyone's expectations will be too high.

If you have a lame date (and you're bound to have a few since that's the nature of dating), think of it as one more crazy dating tale to add to your repertoire. Trust me, when you're in a long-term relationship, this is the stuff you'll want to remember.

NEVER FRIEND A CRUSH ON FACEBOOK

ANDREA

Facebook may be one the best things that's happened to courtship since the invention of Spanx.

Think about it. You meet a cute guy at a party, and even though you didn't exchange phone numbers, you can ping him on one of your social networks and stay connected. You can keep in touch without seeming like you're coming on too strong. And if you really did have a spark, he'll likely be more intrigued when he sees you in your virtual element. Where else can you create a world where you have a great hair day every day and each activity you do sounds interesting and fun?

Another benefit of following or friending a crush online is that you can collect a little more information on your crush's network, sense of humor, and lifestyle. Just remember that though these networks offer a great window into someone's world, real connection and chemistry take time and experience to develop. These networks were not created for us to avoid connecting with people in "real" life. The hope is that with enough virtual engagement, you can build on that momentum and make a plan offline.

A word of caution: beware appearing as if you look at your crush's page as often as you do. Therefore don't say something like, "Hey, Jake. I saw you tried Le Taco Restaurant the other day. How was it? Must've been tiring to drink so many margaritas and play softball the next day. Looks like you had a busy weekend!"

Instead, use social networks as a platform for flirting. Share a witty comment on your crush's wall (sparingly), or like one of his adorable photos. Invite him to events you create, and keep your interactions light. Use it as a casual way to stay connected, and it's a win-win for all.

When not to follow or friend

Facebook is a wonderful way to access a new crush; however, if you're already in the beginning phases of dating someone, I'd recommend staying off of his Facebook (or Twitter or foursquare or Instagram or Vine) page. Unless you want to spend time overanalyzing why your date went out Friday night, when he said he was busy working, or who the cute gal on his arm is in a party photo, steer clear of friending, following, or poking while your status is still single.

Putting aside the merits of Spanx, I'm anti-Facebook courtship. Friend-flirting can cause several problems—namely, jealousy, insecurity, and something I like to call ROOD, or Romantic Overload of Data. (Once again, I've never actually called it that.)

With ROOD, you immediately know their favorite books and favorite music, you've seen photos of their trip to Budapest, and you have a running digital diary of their life. This saps the fun from the getting-to-know-you process. Even an innocent question, like "When are you free next week?" can get complicated, as you post an update, and he thinks, *Hey, how come her status update says she's at happy hour? I thought she had to work late!*

So, if possible, avoid Facebook. (I do agree with Andrea that if you just met, Facebook is an acceptable—not ideal, but acceptable—medium for getting in touch.) And if you become friends, "Like" judiciously, flirt publicly at your own peril, think twice about tagging photos, and remember that PDA on Facebook walls is tacky at best and barfy at worst. If you're happily in love? Good for you, really happy for you. But please don't gush about it on Facebook . . . not for your sake, but for the rest of your friends. This is an actual Facebook post from an actual friend-of-a-friend, posted, ironically enough, while I was working on this chapter:

> One year ago today, I took a chance on a blind online date with a guy who most girls would have written off as an internet stalker. . . . It was something about the words he wrote to me (okay, and maybe the blond hair, the twinkling blue eyes and the possibility of him actually being over six feet tall) that intrigued me and gave me the courage to meet him for dinner. . . . From that very first encounter, I knew he was something special and I wanted so very much to be a part of him. . . . Today I can't imagine sharing my heart with anyone else, and I am so grateful for the amazing partnership, friendship and love we have found in each other! I love you, Ken!

Please don't do this. Thank you.

Q: Should you cyber-search
before the first date?

JEFF

Last week you met someone at a bar. He's cute, he's funny, and you're going out tomorrow night. He handed you his business card, and he has a unique name, Paco Valenti. There can't be that many Paco Valentis. If you search his name you're bound to get, at the very least, Facebook, LinkedIn, and the ranking of his seventh-grade soccer team.

You're tempted. But you feel a little stalkery. Do you cyber-search him?

The case for it:

Maybe he's a nut job, has a criminal record or, worse, says his favorite book is *Fifty Shades of Grey*. These are things you have a right to know. Or, more likely, maybe you find a few pics of Paco, which will clarify whether he's as hot as you remembered or if you were just really, really drunk. Besides, he's probably searching the internet for you, right? Tit for tat.

The case against it:

It feels dirty. It feels like you cheated. Instead of getting to know the person organically, you're allowing your impressions to be framed by their online persona. We've all done embarrassing things, and like it or not, those embarrassing things are sometimes chronicled—and preserved for eternity—on the first page of Google search results. Employ the Golden e-Rule, which is as useful as it is clichéd: if you'd rather not be e-judged, don't e-judge your date.

This is all nice in theory. In reality? Almost all of us do it. Pre-date internet searches are no longer taboo. They're prevalent. It's not weird to search for someone, but it's weird to *tell them* you did, or to reference something specific from their past. We've reached an unspoken policy of "Don't Ask, Don't Tell."

Unless his favorite book really is *Fifty Shades of Grey*. Don't ask, don't tell, just...run away.

Beware of What You Read Online

ANDREA

My name, Andrea Syrtash, is both a blessing and a curse. As far as I know, I'm the only one with it. (My father made up our surname, which is too long a story to print here, but let's just say he thought "Syrtash" sounded cool and western when he moved to Canada from Hungary.)

Bad photos, fun interviews, and random factoids from my past pop up when you search for me online. It's a virtual "this is your life" hodgepodge. I write for a number of online media outlets and try not to read user comments. (Getting called an idiot and a whore is fun the first few times, but it gets old fast! Really, though, I may never get used to hateful comments by strangers, and I find this aspect of the World Wide Web fascinating. And scary.)

Recently, I filmed a segment with "The Shine" on Yahoo! about how to keep marriage fun, fresh, and fulfilling. I didn't read the twenty-five hundred comments about me and my advice, but a friend brought something to my attention with the subject line "Your three ex-husbands..."

A user named "Willow" weighed in about me on Yahoo's message board. He (or she?) wrote, "People working on their third marriage should not be labeled 'experts'!" When probed by others and asked for more information on my relationship history, Willow stated the names of my (fake) ex-husbands. He/she wrote, "[Andrea] was married to Robert C. Schink, divorced 2010; Jeffrey Dubois, divorced 2008; and finally,

Steven A. Smith, divorced 2005. She makes thirty-nine thousand dollars a year in alimony . . . pretty good work if you can find it."

First of all, Willow is bad at math — because Michael would be my fourth husband in this case. More important, though, Willow reminds us that you simply can't believe everything you read online.

IF HE'S INTO YOU, HE'LL CALL (NOT TEXT)

JEFF

About a year ago, as research for a different project we collaborated on, Andrea and I combed the bars, restaurants, and streets of New York to ask men and women questions about dating. We covered lots of topics — turnoffs, cheating, sex, the works — but there was one subject, in particular, that caused the most confusion: *to call or to text?*

Here's the irony. Plenty of guys told us, "No, no, no, no, trust me! Girls these days . . . they don't like talking on the phone. They want texts," when in the same restaurant, three tables over, women told us, "Yeah, I like texting, but I still appreciate it when a guy makes the call."

There's an asymmetry of information. Men *think* that women prefer texts, when actually, especially in the early phase, they usually want the courtesy of a call. Texting is such a cheap form of communication. A phone call takes guts. A phone call, at the very least, is a guy's way of saying, "I like you enough to give you more than thirteen seconds of my time."

The takeaway? During the first couple of dates, if you, as a woman, are frustrated because the guy always texts, part of the reason, potentially, is that *he thinks that's what you want.* The issue is a lack of knowledge, not a lack of interest.

Here's one thing that you can do, and file this under So Crazy It Just Might Work. You can actually—it's crazy!—discuss whether you prefer phone or texts. It doesn't have to be a Big Serious Talk. It can be casual, and it can come up organically on the second or even the first date: "Are you a phone person or a text person?" Problem solved.

While we're on the subject, let's look at some of the worst text offenders:

> Text Message
>
> YOU AROUND FRIDAY NIGHT?

ISN'T THIS ANNOYING? WHY ARE WE SHOUTING? I will vote for the next Presidential Candidate that promises to abolish All-Caps.

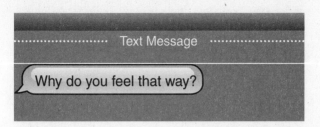

Texts are good for the Whens, Whats, and "Hi"s. Not so much for the Whys.

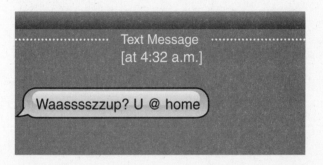

Maybe after midnight, phones should require Breathalyzers?

[at 10:59 p.m.]

Where are you? What's going on?

[at 11:32 p.m.]

WHERE ARE YOU?!

Kristy sent these texts—or some just like it—to her boyfriend, and they never really recovered. (Clarification: I'm not suggesting women are more prone to doing this than men. Guys do it, too.) Not everyone checks their phone at all times, and the lack of a five-minute response does not, necessarily, mean he's boffing his secretary. (Kristy's boyfriend was seeing a movie.)

One final thought, and it's the recurring theme of the book: if you and the guy are a good match and have chemistry, *it doesn't really matter* if you call, text, email, fax, or communicate through chat messaging in Words With Friends.* The corollary: if you and the guy *don't click*, then it also doesn't really matter. No decision about call vs. text, no matter how impeccably made, can salvage a vibe that's only mediocre.

---

* It's time to add Words With Friends to the list of confusing communication channels. When you're spelling words with double entendres, this can be awkward. Quick case study: I was playing a game with a woman I found really attractive, flirting with her over the in-game chat. Then, insulted, she called me out on the last two words I'd played without even thinking, "cow"... and "oink." *Oops.* Smooooooth.

> Q: When should I take my online dating profile down?

ANDREA

No matter how much you've dated or how savvy you are in life, there will be times when you revert to an awkward seventh-grade girl at the start of dating someone new. Don't worry. Great, confident men also transform into prepubescent boys when they're interested in you. With that comforting preface, I will offer this advice:

There comes a time in a modern dater's life when she has to make sure her virtual life and her real life align. We live in a digital world, and at some point someone who's into you may dig around (read "e-stalk") to learn more about your relationship status and to try to assess whether or not you're into him. You'll engage in this creepy online behavior, too, of course.

Knowing when to take your online dating profile down is tricky. You don't want to be presumptuous and have a big "Let's remove all our dating profiles!" discussion, but you also don't want to stay on three sites for singles if you've started to date someone exclusively. Keeping your online dating profile up while you're in a relationship is equivalent to hanging out at a bar solo, looking supercute and available. You'll get approached.

When Michael and I started dating more seriously, a friend told me that she spotted his profile on JDate. My first reaction was, "Forget him! I'm outta here!" but I played it cool as a cucumber. Instead of freaking out with twenty questions, I simply said to him,

(continued)

"My friend almost picked you up on JDate last night! She liked your write-up...." (Yay for being passive-aggressive!) I kept it light and casual, but he got the point and responded that he hadn't logged in in weeks. He opened his computer right there and deleted the profile.

If you want to bring up the "Why are you still on a dating site?" question, you can also take a silly approach with something like, "I just took down my OkCupid profile, since I'm sick of not paying for a dating site" or "Well, it's been fun to meet super creepy dudes...I think I'm ready to cancel my membership."

However you communicate your virtual needs, just make sure you're not putting him on the defensive. There are no hard and fast rules on how to navigate these awkward moments in the life of a new relationship. There's also a good chance that being on the site (or not being on the site) didn't even occur to him.

JEFF

What's the most awkward part of online dating? It's not the cyber-messaging, it's not seeing them in person, and it's not even fumbling to answer the "How'd you guys meet?" question at your wedding. The trickiest part is when you *really hit it off* with someone...but wonder if they're still playing the digital field.

This is different from normal dating. Or, more accurately, it takes a question that always existed in dating—"Is he/she interested in me or someone else?"—and hyper-amplifies it, thanks to the twin forces of hyper-connectivity and hyper-transparency.

Hyper-connectivity

Match, JDate, eHarmony, OkCupid, and SoSoCupid all have apps for your smartphone. This means that you *always* have instant access to a bottomless pool of romance. More concretely, it means that you're constantly, neurotically checking your phone to see who trolls your page. So you can be trapped in a conference room at work, nodding as your boss reviews the company's inventory goals, while you discreetly view photos of an 89 percent match. (I've done this.) You check your phone before you roll out of bed. You check your phone at the bar. Here's where it gets weird: you can even check your smartphone *while you're on a date.*

It's addictive. When you're in the throes of online dating, you simply *can't help* checking your page to see what else is out there. It takes the crack-like qualities of Facebook and multiplies them by a thousand, powered by the rocket fuel of sex and romance.

Hyper-transparency

Hyper-connectivity gets problematic when you combine it with the second issue: hyper-transparency. Dating sites keep track of when you go online, and they display this for all your potential suitors to see, and they even flash Online Now! when you're just quickly checking the app on your phone. Yikes. This means that when you go on a date with someone you met online, after the date, they can check your profile page to see if you've been cyber-trolling.

I once had an OkCupid first date that went exceptionally well. She was smart, dynamic, funny, yada yada. I left her place at 4 a.m.

(continued)

after a sprawling, seven-hour conversation and heavy make-out session. I floated home. The next morning I checked OkCupid from my phone, like always, and saw that she was last online at 2:30 a.m. Wait, we were making out at 2:30! Did she literally check OkCupid while her tongue was in my throat? Maybe she waited until I was in the bathroom. Or maybe her computer was on in the other room. It doesn't really matter. The point is that when you first start dating someone that you met online, you have to play some Game Theory—who will stop peeking first?

So when do you say, "Enough's enough, let's end the addiction, let's take down our profiles?" There's no magic timeline, but this is how it usually works: you do it when you begin to forget that you're even on the website. You'll no longer check OkCupid before rolling out of bed. You'll go days and then weeks without even thinking about it. At that point you should take it down.

And instead of *insisting* that the guy take it down, you can just tell him matter-of-factly that yours is down. "Hey, no pressure, but just FYI, I took down my Match profile." He either will or will not take down his. And if he doesn't and it's been two months, why waste your time, right?

To Call or to Text?

"I usually date women in their midtwenties to early thirties, and I usually text. I get the feeling that texting is usually more comfortable for all involved." —Matt

"Call if you give a shit. Text if you want to keep it casual and/or hook up. Calling is a big deal these days and sends a signal of genuine interest in two-way conversation. Also, it builds live rapport in a way that texting cannot." —Teresa

"Call. You can't whisper sweet nothings over texts." —Jackie

"No one calls anymore." —Diane

"Texting is fun. But phone calls are what separates a man from a boy." —Lauren

"If you text me before calling me, I will punch you in the throat." —Michelle

"The song isn't 'Text Me Maybe.'" —Kyle

"You mean phones actually still make calls? How retro!" —Casey

"Both genders prefer text messaging because it eases the pressure and nervousness of the initial courtship. I enjoy getting little text messages during the day and can even find a phone call intrusive." —Teddy

"Old school: Call her, damn it. Texting is for wimps." —Jim

"I hate talking to people on the phone, but it's hard to text and be witty in so few characters." —Devin

"If he's funny, a good writer, and has basic etiquette skills and common sense, then texts could possibly work, but a 3 a.m. 'hey girl where u at' or a 2 a.m. 'can i come over' after not seeing him for five months is the kiss of death." —Elizabeth

"I once met a guy who seemed intelligent, motivated and mature. Great conversation, good dancer. We exchanged numbers. That night, after parting ways, he texted me 'good nite. i wish ur tite little booty was in bed with me rite now.' Suffice it to say, I never contacted him again." — Rochelle

"CAAAALLLLLL!!!" —Lisa

ALWAYS UNFRIEND AN EX

ANDREA

You have two options when you break up with someone who you're on social networks with—you can "unfriend" him or "ignore" him. If unfriending seems too drastic, do yourself a favor and enable the "ignore" function on Facebook, Twitter, foursquare, Google+, Pinterest, Instagram, and any other social media tool that's become wildly popular in the last few minutes. Otherwise, you will obsessively check your ex's updates and question every move, i.e., "Why did Tim check into Angellos Restaurant? That's our place!" or "Who's that idiot he's tagged with? Why is his arm around her waist!" You will make up stories based on 140 characters of information and will become a creepy e-stalker without even realizing it.

> ## Q: When should I change my relationship status on Facebook?

ANDREA

It's better not to specify your relationship status on your profile pages unless you want forty-seven people, including your aunt Betsy, to comment on your dating life or you want to face the awkward "When should I post that we're dating?" question, which inevitably arises in the age of social media announcements.

Ultimately, though, that call is up to you. If you are compelled to scream from the mountaintops (or casually post) that you are Brad's girlfriend, go for it! Just be prepared for questions, comments, and potential (virtual) discomfort should things not work out with Brad. Oh, and first make sure it's okay with Brad before you tag him as your boyfriend.

Whatever you do, don't unilaterally change your relationship status and tag the guy you're seeing if you haven't discussed it first. (BIG no-no.)

And speaking of discussing it...

As with removing your online dating profile, broach the topic casually. Try something like, 'I don't want to poke around with anyone else on Facebook. Do you want to be my Face relationship?" (Okay, please not that, but you get the point.) As long as you make it cute, funny, or sweet, he won't run for the hills. And if he does? Good thing you know now.

JEFF

Keep it simple. Don't broadcast your status on Facebook, period. Done and done.

JEFF

It's an odd feeling to click the "Remove as Friend" button. You used to care about him, you probably still care about him, and suddenly, *zap*, you can't even see the photos he shares with 463 of his closest friends. In a single cyber-second you're demoted from the most important person in his life to…well, not even in his top 463. In some ways this feels more final, more cold, and more depressing than the actual breakup.

But it has to be done. And don't worry about whether it seems rude or hostile; he'll get it. Unfriending just goes with the breakup territory. When I'm on the receiving end of the unfriending (not uncommon!), my first reaction is hurt and sadness and regret, and then I realize she did the right thing.

Breakups need space. Even if you're destined to eventually "just be friends," in the immediate aftermath there's no upside to reading his status updates, seeing where he checks in on foursquare, or studying every photo for the telltale signs of a new girlfriend.

Exception 1:
If the ex is someone from the past? Different story.
If you've both moved on and you're legitimately just friends, go ahead and be friends.

Exception 2:

Once every 137 years, there's a couple that has a super-amicable breakup, where both parties are mature, unresentful, and cool with the new status. No need to unfriend. (If you're not sure if you're in this category, you're not.)

Let's Talk About Sex(ting): Ten Quick Thoughts

1. **No abbreviations.**

   "I'm hot for you" loses moxie when spelled "Hot 4u."

2. **Never sext before sex.**

   Scientific fact: if you sext someone before you've even kissed, there's a 97 percent chance that you will never hear from them again.

3. **Make sure it's someone you trust.**

   We live in an age of digital footprints. Your texts, photos, and videos can haunt you for decades.

4. **A little goes a long way.**

   Go easy on the frequency. Too many and you both become desensitized.

5. **Tease.**

   Let's say you want to send a racy picture. Begin with something suggestive but not overly revealing. (Think plunging neckline.) If your first pic's a full frontal, where can you possibly go from there? Never mind, we don't want to know. (Or half of us do. Feel free to email these to Jeff.)

6. **Start by feeling things out.**

   How do you begin this awkward digital dance? One angle: Start with something ambiguous that can play out either way. Something like "Crazy dream about you last night . . ." does the trick. If they respond, "Ooooh, tell me more," then game on. And maybe holster the phone if they respond with, "Um . . . I have to go."

7. **Leave something to the imagination.**

   There's a reason lingerie is hot. It's provocative, but it forces you to want just a *little* more. Good sexts do the same.

8. **Laugh. Flirt.**

   Have a sense of humor about it. And sexting doesn't have to be vulgar or X-rated; mildly erotic flirts can be just enough to add spice.

9. **Try it sober.**

   It's tempting to sext only at 2 a.m., when both parties are drunk and less inhibited. But there's something extra-provocative about a hot text at 10:30 a.m. on a Tuesday (provided you've already sexted before). That said . . .

10. **Consider the context.**

    Be respectful of real-life boundaries. If your partner has a work-issued BlackBerry, usually, it's best to avoid sending them pictures of your genitalia.

Chapter 5
SEX

A sneak peek into our writing process... When a man and a woman are cowriting a dating book and talking—professionally—about sex in a coffee shop, they will get some funny looks. It's hard to keep a straight face when saying, "Hey, should blow job be one or two words?"

- Seal the deal with a kiss
- Bad kisser = Bad chemistry
- Break it off if the sex is bad
- Don't talk about "your number"

SEAL THE DEAL WITH A KISS

JEFF

A lot of guys think that if a first date doesn't end with a kiss, it's not really a date. And by "a lot of guys" I mean, well, me.

I'm sort of kidding, but not really. To figure out whether we should go for the kiss, men have subconsciously invented what I'll call the Kissing Matrix. For men, this is one of those rare, beautiful times when everything is simple.

The Kissing Matrix looks at the possible outcomes of two intersecting variables:

1. If the guy kisses her.
2. If the woman wants to be kissed.

When you break down the four possible outcomes from the guy's perspective, the only logical move is crystal clear.

	Kiss Her	Don't Kiss Her
She Wants You to Kiss Her	1. Success.	2. She wonders you're either a) uninterested or b) a wimp.
She Doesn't Want You to Kiss Her	3. You will never see her again.	4. You will never see her again.

If the guy kisses her and she wants him to kiss her—quadrant 1—success. Easy call.

If she doesn't want the guy to kiss her—quadrants 3 and 4— the outcomes are identical. Put differently, if she's not feeling the vibe, *it doesn't matter* if the guy kisses her or not. It's a dead end either way.

From the guy's perspective, she has no reason to be upset, shocked, or indignant. A first-date kiss is not breaking any rules or overstepping bounds or violating her trust. It's a *date*. This is what people do. If the guy makes his move and she jukes her head in protest, the guy says he's sorry, laughs it off, and knows that he plays his odds. (Think about blackjack. You always double down on eleven. Even though you don't win every hand, doubling is the right move, the smart move, the only move.) So if there's a spark, the guy has every reason to see where it will lead. Maybe nowhere. Or maybe somewhere amazing and special and magical, like her apartment.

You might be thinking, *But wait! What if she had a great time and had an amazing first date, but she simply doesn't want to kiss?* That's not even a mathematical outcome that we men understand. Our brains can't compute.

ANDREA

Jeff and I differ on this one. I think if you had a good connection on the date, you're not going to screw that up based on whether or not you kiss at the end of it.

There are plenty of men I've liked in the past that I didn't kiss or sleep with instantly because it just didn't feel right at the time. In one case, a guy was home visiting his family, and his father was down the street, walking the dog, when we pulled up in the driveway. Not sure about you, but I generally don't like to make out while someone's dad is in my line of vision. Sometimes I didn't want to kiss the guy on a first date, because I was still figuring out if we liked each other. And sometimes a kiss hadn't happened, because neither of us had read the cues that we were ready to lock lips.*

Building anticipation by withholding a kiss can be very sexy. Having a hot, steamy kiss can also be very sexy. Just like sleeping with someone on the first date, the bottom line is that you should do what feels good and organic to you in that moment.

---

* Gibberish is commonly spoken moments before a kiss. Blame it on the fact that the first kiss is always a little awkward, but I know that I never spoke so much about the weather, the details of a man's car or career, or any number of random topics as I did before I was ready to make out.

Q: Is it possible to have no-strings-
attached sex?

JEFF

The F-buddy dynamic begins in one of three ways:

1. You have a platonic friend that you hook up with.
   This rarely happens before 2 a.m., and almost
   certainly happens with a greater than .12 blood
   alcohol content.
2. You go on a romantic date, and this relationship
   evolves (devolves?) into strictly casual sex.
3. You're a creeper who trolls for sex on Craigslist.

Ironically, the Craigslist Creeper has the best odds of making an
F-buddy last, as at least the stakes are clear and no one has a hidden
agenda. What you see is what you get. In the case of your platonic
friend? You've probably just destroyed your friendship.

This isn't to say, puritanically, that thou shalt not have an
F-buddy. It can work fleetingly. And if you and your buddy have
crystal-clear transparency—a must—go for it, but just know that
the way you feel today is not the way you, or he, will feel tomorrow.
This can have consequences.

Emotions will, inevitably, slither into the relationship. This can't
be helped. What happens when he gets a girlfriend or when you
get a boyfriend? What if, after sex, he wants to talk about his day,
and you want to call this cute guy you met at the gym? Would he

(continued)

be cool with that, *really?* Human Relationships 101: When you constantly see someone naked, you will eventually feel differently about them, unless you're a proctologist.

ANDREA

Is there such a thing as no-strings-attached sex? According to a number of women I asked this question to recently, the answer is yes. According to Mila Kunis, who starred in *Friends with Benefits*, no. Kunis told GQ in 2011, "It's like communism—good in theory, [but] in execution it fails. Friends of mine have done it, and it never ends well. Why do people put themselves through that torture?"

My friend Matt disagrees with Mila (though he'd like me to add that he finds her lovely). He's enjoyed the benefits of a no-strings hookup. In Matt's words:

Right before I moved to Los Angeles, I was having a late-night texting conversation with a friend of mine. It was quickly becoming flirtatious in a fun way. After a few minutes, I put it out there that we should get together for the night. We quickly set the ground rules like a business negotiation. "This is a one-time deal. No spending the night. Must use protection. This is our little goodbye." After a very fun night in bed, she said to me, "So... should I write you a recommendation letter for the women in LA?" That was four years ago. We are still friends and talk often. If you set the rules, it will work... and it can be hot!

Whether it's a friends-with-benefits arrangement or a just-for-fun fuck buddy, before you get laid, it's worth laying down some ground rules. The boundaries should be set not only for the person you are shagging, but also for yourself. If you're unsure if you can handle this arrangement, ask yourself:

1. What's my motivation in having noncommittal sex? What do I hope to get out of this arrangement? Is it to satisfy my hormones or to satisfy a deeper longing? (Be honest about your true intentions.)
2. Will this prevent me from meeting and dating other men that I could have a relationship with? What choices will I make if I meet someone I see potential with? (These questions are only for those of you who are interested in a relationship, of course!)
3. How will I feel if the guy I'm hooking up with can't make it to my place one night because he's taking another woman out?

Once you're clear about your intentions, communicate them to your F-buddy. Don't want him to come to you after a hot date with someone else? Want him to tell you if he's started sleeping with another person? Don't want to be cuddled after sex? Let him know what you need, and be open to what he has to say.

Set boundaries for yourself, as well. If you start to develop feelings for and an attachment to your no-strings-attached guy, make sure you're able to cut off the relationship, instead of hoping he'll come around and see how great you are. (You are great—I promise—but it's rarely a good idea to stick around, trying to convince someone of this fact!)

More and more women are looking to get their sexual needs fulfilled without the commitment and work of a relationship. I spoke with one 37-year-old attractive woman who proudly told me that she's turned off when a man she just wants to hook up with gets too needy. "I just want to have sex without feelings getting in the way. Why is that so hard to believe?"

BAD KISSER = BAD CHEMISTRY

ANDREA

My friend David really liked Aly but couldn't get over her "lizard lips." He told me her lips were thin, dry, and scaly. A month later he dated "the hygienist" (she apparently earned the nickname because he needed a suction to release all the saliva she transferred into his mouth). David didn't ask either woman out for another date, because he felt there was no way they could have chemistry if they didn't have kissing chemistry.

A bad kiss may feel like a deal breaker, but keep in mind that it's a lot easier to alter someone's kissing style than change his personality. Sometimes you don't think you like the way someone kisses because you're used to the lips of the last person you dated, and sometimes you have to teach your date how to kiss you correctly. Kissing is an interactive experience: your date needs your participation for it to work.

If your date's sucking the life out of your lips when he plants a kiss on you at the end of the night, you can slow down the pace and *show* him how you want to be kissed. When he kisses you in a way that works for you, encourage him with your body language.

"Show, don't tell" is generally the best approach when it comes to kissing and sex.

I'm more cynical than Andrea here. Bad kissing is hard to fix. Maybe they force their tongue down your throat and scrub it back and forth, like a toothbrush. Or maybe they keep their mouth closed like a gully fish, put their hands in their pockets, and hope that you'll do the rest. Bad kissing chemistry is a sign of bad overall chemistry, and you either have it or you don't.

My First Kiss

JEFF

In high school I accomplished something truly historic. I was the president of both Junior Statesmen of America (JSA) and our debate team, an unprecedented honor that made me, without question, the biggest geek in the history of my school.

Every year we took a road trip to Austin for the JSA Convention, which could also be called "the big virgin party." We stayed at a glitzy hotel, had Mock Congress and state elections (whooo!), and met the delegates from other schools.

As president of the dorks, I had to meet and mingle. This forced me out of my shell. And then something miraculous happened: a girl flirted with me. This had never happened before. She had thick, meaty shoulders and her breath smelled like too much cinnamon gum, but she was a real live girl, and she flirted with me.

Maybe she was spellbound by the power of my dual presidency. Maybe she was as lonely as me. I don't know. But somehow within the first hour of courtship, we found ourselves alone in a hallway, while the rest of the dorkiticians were at the Kool-Aid mixer.

She gives me a kiss. My first kiss. Her breath is warm and cinnamony and unpleasant. But, hey, there's another tongue in my mouth. Two tongues! This is great. We kiss more and soon we're petting.

She grabs my hand, pumps it, and yanks me down the hallway. "Where are we going?"

"To my room." She presses her mouth to mine, hard.

Jesus. We get to her room. Her roommates are all downstairs at the mixer. We do some more stuff. My hands fumble with a thick, cottony grandma bra that just might stop bullets. I have no idea what I'm doing, and after a few moments we're sitting face-to-face with both of our legs spread open in a wide V, my thighs on hers. This little maneuver — the Interlocking V — is awkward and gives neither of us leverage and should never be performed again by anyone, anywhere, ever.

We kiss some more, me still not believing my luck. Any normal, well-adjusted, experienced guy my age would take this moment for what it was, enjoy it, maybe go to second or even third base.

I lacked that sophistication. This was not just my first kiss of high school; this was my only kiss. This was my chance. I acted on what both Martin Luther King, Jr. and President

Obama called "the fierce urgency of now." I kiss her, tell her that I'll go downstairs to the hotel store, buy condoms, and come back. She nods her head, urgent.

I sprint out of the hotel room. I bolt down God knows how many flights of stairs. I get to the hotel gift shop...two minutes after they close. *Damn it. This isn't happening. No. They have to be open.*

It's a glass wall, and I can see a woman still inside, counting the register.

I knock on the glass door. She can see me, but she just shakes her head.

I knock again. I plead with my eyes.

She ignores me.

Desperate times...I knock again and then whisper, "Condoms."

She looks up, but she can't hear me.

I raise my voice and cup my mouth. "Condoms! I need to buy a box of condoms, please."

It still doesn't get through. I raise my voice, and I yell loud enough for her to hear me through the glass wall, "Condoms! It's an emergency!"

She just points to the register. Closed.

I wave a ten-dollar bill. *Please, please, please—*

She finally looks up and takes in my desperate condition. I'm wearing an ill-fitting suit, yellow-tinted glasses, and this is clearly the only chance I've ever had to see a girl naked. I must have given off that vibe. She tries to hide a smile, opens the door, takes my cash, and gives me a box of condoms. Yes!

I sprint up the stairs. I dash past the third floor, the fourth floor. *Damn it. What floor is she on? No. No, no, no. Maybe the sixth floor, right?*

I get to the sixth floor and jog through the halls, hoping to find a landmark. *Let's see, she was in room number... five-something. Or maybe six-something. Three-something. Oh no. Room five-forty-two? Room three-fifty-seven? Jesus.* This is a time before cell phones, I don't know her room number, and I don't even know her last name.

I roam the hallways for another hour. Nothing. She's gone. I never saw her again.

BREAK IT OFF IF THE SEX IS BAD

ANDREA

This is one we hear all the time: bad sex is a deal breaker. But is it really? I don't think so. Is lack of passion and chemistry a deal breaker? I think so. What's the difference? I'll explain.

It's not uncommon to have a certain period of adjustment with a new sexual partner and have to get used to his moves, his scent, his taste, and his approach in the bedroom. If you've recently dated someone who likes aggressive and wild sex and you're now with a partner who wants to stare longingly into your eyes and move slowly and steadily, it may take some getting used to (or it may take time to figure out how to encourage your new partner to do what you like in bed).

So often we call sex bad when it's just awkward and we haven't found our rhythm yet. You may be wildly attracted to your date but wish he would try some new moves between the sheets. That kind of "bad sex" is easy to fix. If you have good chemistry otherwise, it may just be a matter of a little time and practice (it's the good kind of homework!) to turn that bad sex around.

As I mentioned earlier, a "show, don't tell" approach is generally best. Rather than saying, "I hate it when you . . . ," try encouraging your partner with words or sounds when he does something you like. He'll want to get that reaction again.

If, however, you are dating someone and find yourself running through your to-do list every time you guys make out, you may not have a physical spark. Trust me, I've been in this situation with a handsome and totally awesome guy, and it stinks to feel nothing (but boredom) when someone you want to be with is touching you.

I'll never forget how I felt when the very cute guy I was dating, Seymour,* touched me. Not only did I not get turned on, I found myself turned off. I hated his touch, his breath, and his moves. How could a man that attractive be so unattractive in bed?

If you're in a monogamous relationship, the reality is that sex is one thing that you can't get elsewhere. You can be happy in a relationship with someone who doesn't like art, as you can

---

* Seymour is not his real name. Do you really think I'd reveal the name of a guy who's bad in bed in a book? Do you really think I'd date a guy named Seymour?

recruit a friend to join you at a new gallery when you want to go, but if you're with someone who you don't want to be physically intimate with (or who doesn't want to be physically intimate with you), you can't recruit a friend to fulfill your needs (unless you're looking to cheat on your partner, which is a different book).

It's one thing to discover you don't enjoy sex with someone you've been dating for a few months. It's a different story if he's someone you've been with for many years—who you love and want to build a future with. If it's more serious, I'd suggest looking at all the resources available to you—sex therapy, couples retreats and workshops, books, DVDs, and online kits. Don't make it a deal breaker unless you're sure that you've exhausted all resources or you decide it's something you can live with since everything else clicks.

JEFF

I agree with Andrea. It's a deal breaker when you *don't want* to have sex with the person. Do you have no desire to see them naked? Does the thought of making out with them give you the willies? This is a real problem, and it's a problem that alcohol can solve only temporarily.

Unlike kissing, sex can get better with time. The first few encounters can be awkward, and you eventually learn each other's turn-ons and turnoffs. (Maybe she's into blindfolds, but he's into furry toys—that's just not the type of thing you discover on Date One.)

You should know that from the guy's perspective, there's almost no such thing as bad sex. That's like saying "bad money" or "a bad win." It's Gender Inequity #837. It's usually pretty easy for guys to get off. (Just in case there's ever a woman out there who's insecure about how she is in the sack, let me say this right now: There's no need to worry. Trust me, you're great at sex. You're the best. From the guy's perspective, it's *almost impossible* not to be good at sex. To be bad at sex, a woman would have to cry uncontrollably, fall asleep [while snoring], or slap us with the remote control. And even then…some guys probably have that fetish. Trust me. You're good at sex.*)

And what if the guy never gives you the Big O? Like, never? This depends on the context, on how long you've been dating, and also, most important, on how the guy reacts. Does he have a good sense of humor and show a willingness to do something different, to be more responsive, to mix things up, to give you what you need? Or is he sex-selfish? His reaction matters. If he's willing to make an effort—and if everything else in your relationship clicks—then there's reason for optimism. If he's a boorish oaf who falls asleep after finishing and doesn't even see the problem, well, yeah, that's a bright red unsexy flag.

---

* Unless you're related to me, in which case I assume that you have never even thought about sex, ever. Please rip this page and burn it.

> ## Q: How do I talk dirty?

ANDREA

Let's start with how *not* to do it. Generally speaking, high-pitched baby talk, using so many crass words that you sound like you're on the air with Howard Stern, or nicknaming every one of his body parts cutesy names like "peanut" is not a turn-on, but almost everything else is fair game in the bedroom, depending on your comfort level.

The truth about dirty talk is that it's not necessarily about what you say, but about how you say it. Saying "I want you inside of me" with a nervous giggle isn't nearly as sexy as saying it by whispering the same words in his ear. If you're not feeling verbal, consider the fact that moans and groans are often as sexy as words during sex. And the opposite is true: one of my guy friends said one of his weirdest sex experiences happened with a woman he was dating who didn't move or make a peep. When they'd get it on, he wasn't even sure that she was awake.

Other things to keep in mind: Compliments and positive feedback are good (i.e., "I love it when you . . ."), but remember that sex talk can be too graphic. If you're too detailed about what is happening, you can both be taken out of the moment. Nobody needs a play-by-play account of what he's doing, what you're doing, what you want, what's working, what you hope to try. Subtle and suggestive is sexy.

JEFF

Don't worry. I won't write about *how* you should talk dirty, as that would embarrass you and me both. (Although I'm tempted to write something totally crass, just to see what it sounds like in the audiobook. *Cock. Vagina.*)

But here's the crux of the issue: How do you start it? If no one's done it yet, who has the guts to go first? This is the usual anxiety (felt by both men and women). We all worry, *What if what I say sounds silly? What if he won't shut up? Will this sound like a bad porno?*

So given all that confusion, I will say this. There has never, ever, ever been a case where a woman talked dirty and I didn't like it. That's never happened. Dirty talk is sexy, period. In other words, if you take a risk and go for it—no matter what you say!—it will almost always be appreciated . . . and then reciprocated.

Men like reassurances in the sack. It's nice to hear that we're doing a good job, so dirty talk is just one way, of many, to show him that you're having a good time. And the more you're into it, the more he's into it—it's a positive feedback loop, like the circle of life.

Talking about Dirty Talk

Shockingly, most of our other friends and interviewees didn't want to talk dirty to us when we were collecting quotes.

"Worst dirty talk I've ever experienced? This is mid-sex: 'You know, I've been with a girl before who has tits a lot like yours…but yours are better.' Ultimately, I'm yea for dirty talk. Just *good* dirty talk. Not dirty talk about another girl's boobs. And how closely you've dissected mine." —Lauren

"I like to get dirty talk going with a question. If I ask, 'Do you like that?' and she says, 'Uh-huh,' I'll back off, but I'm more likely to get a response like, 'Oh, yeah, I love when you do that…. Do you like it?' and we are off to the dirty-talking races." —Dave

"The most awkward dirty talk is when you say, 'What?' because you didn't hear what was said. Repeating the line then sounds, well…not quite right." —Janene

DON'T TALK ABOUT "YOUR NUMBER"

JEFF

Pop quiz: For heterosexual couples, on average, how many more sexual partners would you guess the "average man" has than the "average woman"?

Answer: 0.

The numbers are identical. They have to be. No matter how you slice it, logically, the numbers will always work out to be the same: if a man has sex with seven different women, then those seven women, by definition, had sex. Yet in survey after survey, the "average man" reports having more partners than women, which means that one or both genders are lying.

But does any of this matter? Before having sex, we all have a right to certain data: whether the person has any STDs. That's it. That's all we need to know, and that's all we *should* know.

The issue isn't that we're scared of the answer—well, maybe we're a little scared—but it has to do with the difference between the abstract and the concrete. There are many, many things about women that I know, at some level, in the abstract but I choose not to think about. Toilet stuff, shaving underarms, yeast infections . . . Did that list make you cringe? Good, that's the point. The abstract isn't a big deal, but specific words, like, say, *taking a dump*, make us all wince. (I'm sorry. I wish you could un-read that, but I had to prove a point.) This is just part of having a human body, and there's obviously nothing wrong with it, but it's best to avoid the specifics.

And of course the opposite is true. Women would be traumatized if they knew how gross men could be if left to their own devices. You know the clichés about how guys are all cavemen, and dress it up only in the company of women? All true. On a camping trip with buddies, the entire weekend was a glorious mix of grunts and flatulence. In the abstract, fine, you can take that—but would you really want to see (or smell) that campfire?

Our sexual histories are like the icky bodily functions. We know they exist, but let's not talk or think about them. We all exercise a bit of make-believe. When we're with someone we care about, we create this illusion that our romantic past is irrelevant, inconsequential, nonexistent.

And you know what? It's not an illusion. When you're with someone, the past really *doesn't* matter. I don't care if a woman has been with five guys or fifteen guys or five hundred guys. (That's a lie. I'd care if it was five hundred guys.) So that brings up the natural question: Do guys care about a woman's number?

I wish I could tell you something uplifting. But that would undermine my larger goal: to tell you the truth.

Honestly? I really *don't* care about her number. I don't want to hear it, but I wouldn't judge her for it. How could I? My number isn't winning any purity prizes.

But some guys judge. And there's a technical word for this in the psychology of relationships: *bullshit*. The Madonna/whore complex exists, and it's ugly, it's unfair, and it's absurd. I know guys who have hooked up with a hundred-plus girls, but if they find out their girlfriend has hooked up with thirty guys, they'll look down at her as promiscuous. It's an unpleasant holdover from a time that was, quite openly, sexist: If a guy sleeps around, he's a stud. If a girl sleeps around, she's a slut. I can't and won't defend this.

So. Back to the original rule. Maybe it's best to follow the lead of Matthew Crawley in *Downton Abbey*. (Spoiler alert.) As Lady Mary apologizes for her tryst with the Turkish diplomat, he says, "You've lived your life, and I've lived mine. None of that matters." (Second spoiler alert: Unlike Matthew Crawley, we advise you to wear a seat belt.)

The question isn't whether or not to talk about your number; the question is, why is it important for you to do so? Is it a safety issue? Or do you want to do it so you can hear about how many times your partner has . . . done it?

When we were dating, I found that every time I started to discuss my sexual past with Michael, we would inevitably (and uncomfortably) change topics. I really don't need to know that one of his exes was a flexible modern dancer. (In fact, I'm annoyed that I know that.)

The reality is that most people you're with want to know that you have experience between the sheets and are desirable to other people, but they don't want to picture you getting hot and heavy with someone other than them. Starting a sentence with "When I used to go down on Jimmy. . ." doesn't usually lead to a very productive or sexy talk.

If you want to discuss your sexual history to reveal any sexual health issues either of you have, it's appropriate to inquire without sharing specifics. "Have you been tested for STDs in the recent past?" is a perfectly appropriate question to ask a new sexual partner.

Is there a sweet spot in terms of the number of sexual partners one has had? I was recently asked that question by a woman who was entering the teens. (I should clarify. She wasn't a teenager. She was 32 years old and had just surpassed the twelve sexual partners mark.)

Personally, I wouldn't want to be with someone who had never been with anybody else — that would feel like far too much pressure. Also, it would make me question if our values were truly aligned and why this person was still a virgin. By the same token, I'd be concerned if I were sleeping with someone who claimed to have the quadruple-digit track record of Ron Jeremy. (I might even be concerned if I were with someone deep into the triple digits.) So my range of comfort is 1–120, I suppose.

> Q: If you're having sex with more than
> one person at once and they're not
> in the same room, do you have to
> tell them?

ANDREA

At the start of dating someone new, it's not uncommon to find yourself in a situation where you or your date is involved with other people outside of the relationship that you've just started to form together. That's the nature of dating, after all. But when it comes to sex, not everyone is comfortable with the idea of sharing.

When you're in the early courtship phase, it's awkward to address questions of monogamy or exclusivity of any kind. For one thing, you don't want to scare your date away, and for another, you don't want to imply *that this is it* while you're still learning about your compatibility.

Some people are okay with the idea of sleeping with multiple people at once (well, not at once), so don't assume that you know your date's perspective. Err on the safe side—literally and figuratively. If you wouldn't want to continue sleeping with the guy you're dating if he's hooking up with others, broach this topic with confidence and candidness. You're an adult, and it's a very mature and adult thing to discuss your sexual status. There's no need for a big, heavy discussion. You can say something straightforward, like, "I generally don't like sleeping with more than one person at once, so if you are, I'd appreciate it if you let me know." Or lighten it up

(continued)

by acknowledging that it's really unsexy and awkward to talk about it, but you're into safe sex.

JEFF

Let's break down the timeline:

Phase 1: The first few dates
Phase 2: Casual dating
Phase 3: You're dating, but you're not sure how casual it is
Phase 4: You have The Talk
Phase 5: You're dating monogamously
Phase 6: Either you break up or one of you dies

Of course, these phases aren't as clean-cut or as sharply defined as, say, the phases of photosynthesis. It's possible to have The Talk on the first date or never to have The Talk or to date casually forever.

But the above timeline is usually how it works. So let's say you're in Phase 3; it's after you've hooked up, but it's before you've had The Talk. By then, you've probably reached an unspoken understanding, of sorts, that the two of you will spend the weekend together, that you'll be in touch every day, and that you'll come to each other's birthdays or funerals.

When you're in this zone, even if you haven't explicitly said that you're monogamous, the two of you are acting like boyfriend/girlfriend, so it's deceitful to try a side dish. You're breaking the spirit, if not the letter, of the law.

But how about the early, early, early phases of the relationship? Phases 1 and 2? Do you owe your partner a complete reckoning?

At some point it's presumptuous. Let's say you hook up with him on the second date. Do you have the moral obligation to tell him, "Hey, just so you know, on Tuesday, I gave Frank a hand job."

Some people do have a rule that they would never sleep with more than one person at the same time. If that's the case, cool, and you should let your partner know ... but if it's your rule, then the burden is on you to bring it up. (By the way, as far as rules go, that's not a bad one.)

Chapter 6
THIS HAS POTENTIAL (DATES 2, 3, 4ISH)

The rules have some very specific things to say about this phase of courtship. The idea of just going with the flow, having fun, and trusting your gut? Nope. The rules say you need to be calculating, you need to overthink it. Enough.

- Pretend you're busy if you like him
- "He's just not that into you"
- Don't date others if you see potential in him
- Don't date outside your league
- Opposites attract
- Expect a Saturday night date

PRETEND YOU'RE BUSY IF YOU LIKE HIM

ANDREA

The book *The Rules* references "Melanie," a woman all the men loved. According to the authors, "[Melanie] wore makeup and clothes well and acted elusive." Melanie often acted indifferent toward men she liked, sometimes nice, sometimes aloof.

The authors go on to suggest that if the reader wants to find a guy to marry her, she should often pretend to be busy, too. She should wait a few days to return phone calls and should never accept a Saturday night date invitation after Wednesday.

Even though this advice sounds like it's been plucked straight out of our grandma's "How to act like a lady" dating guide, I still hear women quoting this rule. The guidelines confuse men. One said, "So I don't get it.... I can't ever call a woman on a Thursday to ask if she's around on the weekend? What happened to spontaneity?" This rule is counterintuitive to me as I'm pretty sure that kicking off a relationship by being inauthentic is not the best approach when looking for love. Besides, who's really waiting at home by the phone in 2013? (Who really has a phone at home?)

This rule may have worked for us in high school, or even in 1990, when the book *The Rules* first came out, but most self-assured (read "normal") guys will run for the hills—or at least into the arms of another, more interested person—if a woman is never available for a date and always takes days to call him back. And, anyway, do you really want to be with a guy who is so insecure that he'll jump at the chance to speak to you after you've disappeared on him or disrespected him? A big part of the dating process relies on momentum. Pretending to be tied up or disinterested may sabotage the connection you've made.

If you're interested in a man and he's pursuing you, it's best to keep encouraging him to pursue you by being receptive, positive, and open. Men need approval as much as women do, and being standoffish generally won't work in your favor.

There's a nugget of truth in this outdated rule, and it's this: men are generally attracted to women who are engaged in their lives and don't appear to focus only on them. If a guy senses a woman is hanging on his every word or building her entire life around a dinner date with him, that sends a big, red "needy girl" flag up and puts him under a lot of pressure, perceived or otherwise.

I'd edit the "Pretend you're busy if you like him" rule to "*Be* busy if you want to find love."

The best thing you can do for your love life is to love your life! Having passions, interests, outlets, and a dynamic schedule inevitably keeps you engaged in life and upbeat—and there's nothing sexier than that. If I could bottle the joie de vivre we emit when we love life, I would. A man can sense it when you aren't relying on him to "complete" you, and generally wants to be part of the interesting life you've carved out. He's also more likely to work to capture your interest because you have interests other than him. Encouraging him to pursue you, while still engaging in your passions outside of your dating life, is a more realistic and more appealing formula than faking busyness.

The Rules instruct women on how to attract men who like the chase. Wouldn't you prefer to attract a man who likes *you?*

JEFF

There's nothing less cool than someone trying to be cool, and this applies to both sexes. Maybe the guy will try to impress you with something like, "On Tuesday nights, I usually go to this secret, password-only hotspot called L'Douche, but sometimes I get a bottle in the VIP room at Fratbag."

As human beings, we're hardwired to want to impress the opposite sex. That will never change. And we think that to impress them, we must prove that we're fabulously busy, popular, in demand. We want to look awesome.

But you can do this without *pretending* to be busy. At the risk of sounding like an after-school special, you can do this by simply being yourself. (Awww.) He will like you for who you are, and if he doesn't, screw him. You have actual interests, you have hobbies, you have things that you care deeply about. Talk about them. When you're being authentic and excited about things that genuinely excite you, we notice.

That said ...

In the early-early phases of the relationship, it's true, no one wants to come across as *too* available. Let's say you go out on Friday night, and this is how it ends:

Him: *I had a great time.*
You: *Me too.*
Him: *When are you free next?*
You: *I have a dentist appointment next month, but other than that, I have no plans.*

Hmm. Not gonna lie. It *is* a turnoff if we think someone's stuck at home every night, watching *Glee* on endless loop. But the solution isn't to *pretend* to be busy. Inauthenticity is easy to sniff out, it can backfire, and it will cause problems later in the relationship. The solution, as Andrea rightly says, is to just BE busy.

Getting down to nuts and bolts, let's look at the scenario where you really have nothing going on, you have no plans, and you think that you have only two options: (a) pretend or (b) seem overeager. There's a Secret Option C. You can take the initiative. You can say, "Thursday works on my end" without fabricating some cool-sounding plans.

Let's make a pact. If you don't pretend to be busy, we won't lie about clubs like L'Douche.

"HE'S JUST NOT THAT INTO YOU"

This rule has the upside of being short, simple, and easy to understand. It has the downside of being wrong. It clashes with a rule of my own: "Be skeptical of any rule that attempts to explain all the nuance of romantic relationships in six words."

Yes, some guys are not that into you. And some guys are that into you...but have their own legitimate issues, doubts, and insecurities. And some guys are not that into you...yet...but might be.

The rule is not wrong because it's *always wrong*. It's wrong because it dramatically oversimplifies male psychology, it nudges women toward a certain kind of guy, and it has the whiff of misogyny.

Let's look at a rule with equal logical force: "Red meat will kill you." If you follow this rule and never eat red meat, then red meat will never kill you, and the rule will never be proven false. Similarly, if you assume that every guy who's iffy is "not that into you" and if you dump them every time, then you will stay safe and you'll never get hurt. (You might also stay single.)

It's possible that red meat will kill you. If you don't cook it, if you eat too much of it, if you get mad cow disease. But it's also possible just to *be careful* with red meat, use your judgment, and assess the risks on a case-by-case basis. Men are like red meat.

You have to evaluate each situation individually, weigh the risks, and consider the context of what he says and what he does.

Not every guy is a player who doesn't call back. Some guys are shy. Some guys are trapped in the "friend zone," and they *really do* respect you as a friend, and they're not sure how to make a move without risking the friendship. Some guys are getting over an ex and they need some time. Some guys are just flat-out bad at dating but great at being a boyfriend. Some guys are commitment-phobic in the beginning, but once they get comfortable with the woman and the relationship, they lose those jitters. And some guys simply are that busy. They're working, volunteering for charity, going out with friends, or maybe writing a book about dating. True story: When I was frantically trying to make deadlines for this book, a woman, who I liked quite a bit, assumed I "just wasn't that into her" because I had to wake up early every morning and write. Sometimes guys are actually—this sounds crazy!—telling the truth.

Slavishly following this rule will lead a woman to a very certain type of guy: aggressive dudes who play with a full-court press. It rewards the Tarzans who power through every obstacle, and it weeds out the guys who are more sensitive, more contemplative, more prone to take their time. True, following this rule will help safeguard you from getting hurt. But it might also keep you from meeting your match.

The rule also presumes that the woman has no real power other than to *stay* or *walk away*, based on the man's actions. It pretends to be empowering, but it's demeaning to its bones. Relationships are complex, a give-and-take, and require the push and pull of both parties. They're not this black and white. Trust your gut, and if you like him—and assuming he hasn't done anything truly dickish (stood you up, ignored your calls, etc.)—give him a chance. And cross your fingers that you don't get mad cow disease.

The premise of *He's Just Not That Into You* is pretty simple: If a guy is interested in you, he will find a way to be with you. If he doesn't, clearly *he's just not that into you*.

It's true that when a guy is interested in you romantically, he will want to court you. He may do out-of-character things, like clean his bathroom or suggest watching the latest episode of *Real Housewives* with you. His friends will know he's a goner—you've captured his heart. You'll secretly know it, too.

Still, one size doesn't fit all when it comes to attraction and courtship. Catch a guy at a bad time in his life—between jobs, a death in the family, a crisis at work—and you may not be his first priority. In this case, he may be into you and may need to attend to responsibilities that existed long before you met. But the authors of *He's Just Not That Into You* say that "busy is a load of crap."

They also say, "He's just not that into you if he's not calling you." (Men know how to use the phone.)

As Jeff previously mentioned, he and I interviewed a number of men and women a couple of years ago about the big phone versus text question. We asked, "If you don't call a woman to ask her out, does that mean you're not interested romantically in her?" Almost 100 percent of the guys we spoke with said that they often text even when they like a woman (and as Jeff noted, some of these guys thought that women preferred it that way). One guy said, "It doesn't matter if I call or text as long as I'm asking her out or checking in. I want to see her...."

A female client once wrote me with the recommendation, "TELL GUYS NOT TO TEXT ME IF THEY WANT TO SEE ME AGAIN." (I assume she was screaming her request.) But the men we spoke with disagreed. It's possible that they're using this as an excuse—do they really not know that most of us would occasionally appreciate a phone call?—but they reported this to us with sincerity and conviction.

The rules of *He's Just Not That Into You* make sense on a meta-level. Namely, if a dude likes you, he'll want to pursue you. You should never be in a position in which you have to convince someone to give you or a relationship with you a chance.

But moving on when the guy you're seeing doesn't respond in a very specific way may sabotage the connection you're building. If he can't get together because he's on a deadline one weekend, or if he sends a quick "thinking of you" email instead of calling to say the same, there's absolutely no reason to believe he's not into you.

It may be true that a guy you like is into you but is too busy to find time to ever hang out, which still presents a problem for you if you're looking for a significant other. In this case, perhaps it's not that he's just not into you. Maybe he's just not the One *for* you.

DON'T DATE OTHERS IF YOU SEE POTENTIAL IN HIM

ANDREA

In February 2012 the U.K.'s *Daily Mail* published a story entitled "The Dating Rule Book Is Being Rewritten with One in Four Single Girls Dating Three Men at a Time and a Third Happy to Propose."

I think that's worthy of repeating: "ONE IN FOUR SINGLE GIRLS DATING THREE MEN AT A TIME!"

The article attracted attention not just in the U.K., but on this side of the pond, as well. Somehow the notion of women dating multiple suitors seemed progressive to some and promiscuous to others. To me, it seemed like common sense.

There are multiple reasons dating multiple people at the start of courtship is a good idea. I'll highlight just a few of them:

1. **It's not a good idea to put all your eggs in one basket if you don't know if they'll hatch.** Okay, bad analogy, but the point is, you don't want to cut yourself off from a potential relationship with another, more suitable match, because you decided on a first date that you had found exactly what you were looking for. The reality is that a charming man who sweeps you off of your feet on date one may turn into an egomaniacal, self-absorbed d-bag by date six. You won't know his true colors without spending more time with him.

2. **Men can sniff it when you're dating other men.** If a guy senses that he's not your only option, he's more likely to pursue you and show you why you don't need the other dudes you're dating. It's human nature—we often want what we can't have. However, don't confuse this idea of having other options with acting standoffish. The men who want you after you've been disrespectful and rude to them aren't generally the self-assured men you want to date. (By the same token, men can sniff it when you've decided he is it and may be your only option. That's a lot of pressure.)

3. **Level the playing field. There's a good chance he's dating others.** You may decide that you want to stay laser focused on this new, wonderful man, but the

reality is that he's probably been dating others while you've realized this (and he has every right to be). Just make sure you're okay with this fact if you make the decision to stop dating others for a chance at a relationship with him....

There's no timeline for when it's appropriate to become monogamous. It should be organic for both of you to come to the conclusion that you want to date exclusively. Generally, you need to spend time and have shared experiences with one person to know if you want to change your relationship status. In the meantime, embrace the nature of dating and be open to other options.

JEFF

Maybe this isn't a "rule," per se, but it's a sneaky undercurrent of romance stories and movies: when our heroine meets Mr. Right, she falls in love and cuts loose the rest of her suitors, and the two of them—after some madcap high jinks!—live happily ever after.

Sometimes that happens, but usually it doesn't. "Potential" is just that. I've potentially won the lottery and potentially climbed Mount Everest and potentially filed my taxes on time. If you feel a spark with someone, great. See where it goes and give it a real shot, but that shouldn't compel you to cancel your dates, stop flirting, and delete your profile on Match. Not yet, anyway.

That kind of *all in!* approach puts too much pressure on the early courtship. Give it time to breathe. If, after a promising first date, you suspect he's The One and focus all your energy on this one dude, it's easy to appear overeager, puff up your own expectations or, worse, to smother.

Think of this like a negotiation. The heart of any negotiation—a job offer, buying a car—is having leverage. Even if you don't really want your second-best option, knowing that you have it will give you more confidence when you ultimately pull the trigger. You won't feel that you're "settling" with option A, because you know you also have a B, C, and D.

Two quick disclaimers:

Disclaimer 1:
Don't date others just for the sake of dating others.
If you just met someone and you're gobsmacked in
love? Go with it. The point is that you're not *required*
to cut off every other option simply because you met
someone new.

Disclaimer 2:
We're talking about the very, very early stages of
courtship, not once you're in a relationship. We have
a hard line against cheating, and that's the kind of game
playing we hate. I'm already dreading the email from
a reader who says, "Hi. My boyfriend of six months
thinks it's weird that I'm still sleeping with three other

guys, but I showed him your book, said you guys okayed it, but he's still pissed at me. What should I do?" (Or if you do have this issue, please send the email to Andrea.)

DON'T DATE OUTSIDE YOUR LEAGUE

ANDREA

Woody Allen once said that we fall in love with someone when we believe we got the better end of the deal.

At a recent event in Manhattan I was talking with a pretty, accomplished woman who told me that she has high standards, and that's why she believes she's still single in her midthirties. She wants to date men in her league. She explained, "I've dated very successful and impressive men in New York. That's just who I'm drawn to." A moment later she added, "Many of them are self-absorbed jerks who have cheated on me...." I asked her, "Is this the kind of 'high standards' you're referring to?" She smiled, understanding what I was getting at.

In this culture, we define success pretty narrowly. A man can have a high-powered job and be a star at work, but not be present, physically or emotionally, for you and your family. Is that success?

My husband Michael's income as a schoolteacher is significantly less than that of the men I dated in the past who had impressive job titles. Michael works with a number of inner-city youths, who have sometimes written him letters to thank him for changing their lives and being a strong mentor. That's my definition of success.

In fact, I wrote a book called *He's Just Not Your Type (And That's a Good Thing)* about the guys we initially overlook since they don't add up on paper checklists. Here's the thing: we're not marrying a piece of paper!

I've often talked about how I thought I wanted to be with a man who made six figures, but it has turned out, I am happiest with a man who is home by six. This shift happened when I revised my checklist of must-haves and went deeper with my criteria. I started to focus on the qualities I wanted a future *partner*, not just a person, to have. Once I did that, my life changed and my dating "luck" improved. I'd encourage you to do the same.

Think of five must-haves in a partner and five "can't stands," and use this list to guide you in dating. Instead of writing the simple criteria, like "tall" or "successful," write the value behind these. What's important about being with someone with these qualities? To feel protected? To feel attracted? Write down this instead. Dig deeper than the superficial stuff, since the superficial stuff changes with time, anyway. . . .

I should stress that revising your criteria and checklist is not about settling for someone you don't want to be with or settling in any way. In fact, I think we're settling when we simply add up trivial stuff on a checklist and don't consider how important those qualities will be in the long term.

I think you should have very high standards before you settle down. Don't settle for less than being attracted to the guy you're with and excited to be around him. Don't settle for less than feeling happy and secure with this person. And never settle for less than feeling like a really good version of yourself. Those things, more than anything, should be nonnegotiables. A guy who doesn't give you them should always be out of your league.

JEFF

My friend Kevin has a dating theory he calls the "step theory."

In Kevin's words:

1. You are on a step.
2. You do not know which one.
3. You should be able to date people on roughly your equivalent step, perhaps up or down a bit.
4. Steps are based on attractiveness, which, honestly, is largely based on looks. But personality and whatnot can also move you up or down a step or two. Other things typically valued by society, such as wealth or fame, can probably move you up or down more.

5. Thus, in order to find out what step you're on, you have to try going above or below your step. If you approach someone who is well above your step, you'll be rebuffed. Well below, it'll feel "too easy."

And when you first think about Kevin's theory, it *does* seem to have at least a smidgen of truth. Think about most of your friends—they're probably on similar steps. Celebrity couples are on the celebrity step. Jerry Springer contestants are on the Springer step. Deities like Aphrodite and Poseidon are on the Greek gods step.

But here's where the theory unravels.

While the step theory (or "dating in your league," whatever you want to call it) might have some power when you look at *other* couples, it loses value when you view the steps from your own perspective.

This is because most of us have no clue what step we're on, as we're either too insecure or too cocky. My buddies have said to me, "Dude, I'd ask her out, but . . . look at me. She's out of my league," when the guy was objectively better looking. Most people are a rotten judge of their own self-worth. The other flaw: there are many reasons why we're "rebuffed" in dating—it could just be that we're on the same step but we're a bad match.

Besides, what if you're right? What if the other person really is seven steps higher on the staircase of dating? What if they're "out of your league"? There's still no harm in giving it a shot.

The steps presuppose that we have the same tastes, the same values, and the same turn-ons, which is almost never the case. Even if—to all outside observers—one person is simply a "much better catch" than the other, not to get too Hallmarky, but if the two people are happy, does anything else matter?

OPPOSITES ATTRACT

JEFF

Human chemistry is a messy thing. It's complicated. And there's no single variable that can explain whether two people will click; it's like trying to predict an election by looking only at the candidates' dental history. The word *opposite* is squishy, problematic. What, exactly, is an opposite? It can mean so many different things:

Physical opposites
The Beauty and the Beast, Catherine Zeta-Jones and Michael Douglas, any woman and Marilyn Manson.
Religious opposites
The Yankees fan and the Red Sox fan.
Class opposites
This is the dramatic hook of every 19th-century romance novel. One's low class, and one's high class. Will these star-crossed lovers ever make it work?

"Energy" opposites

One wants to go out dancing on Friday night, one wants to crash on the couch. An underrated source of tension.

Neatness opposites

One's a man, one's a woman.

Pedigree opposites

Sam and Diane from *Cheers*. Actually, this is a telling case study. We think of them as opposites, but they're both extroverted, quick-witted, attractive, and share the same core values.

It's difficult—almost impossible—to tack down any one element. You can be an opposite in five ways but a clone in seven others. And even if you *could* define *oppositeness*, there's no telling if that makes you more or less drawn to the person. It cuts both ways. Opposites can work or they can fail; non-opposites can work or they can fail. The variable has no predictive power.

Every relationship needs three things:

1. Mutual attraction
2. Chemistry
3. Compatible values

Attraction can be comprised of opposites: tall vs. short, fat vs. skinny. Chemistry can be comprised of opposites: sarcastic vs. earnest, talky vs. quiet. But there's only one thing that *cannot* be opposite—compatible values. If he wants kids and you want to move to Belize to become a ventriloquist, well, good luck with that.

Besides, realistically, why does this even matter? Would you look at some guy and think, *Oh, he's my opposite. I'll be into him,* or *He's so the opposite of me. We'll never work.* You're probably using the word *opposite* as a proxy for something more fundamental—whether you're into the dude in the first place. That's all that matters. Just trust your instincts and let the chips fall where they may.

ANDREA

Nerdy Ross and fashionable Rachel; bohemian Dharma and her zipped-up husband, Greg; and our favorite prehistoric couple, Fred and Wilma Flintstone, provide great comedic moments and dramatic tension because of how mismatched they are. After all, it would be pretty boring to watch TV characters who saw the world the same way and agreed on everything. But in reality do two very different people have a good shot at long-term love? It's a popular notion that *opposites attract.*

I'm sure you have friends or family in their own odd couple arrangement. It's not uncommon to see a pair in which one person is outgoing and another is shy, or a couple that seems physically mismatched. But from my perspective, the way we judge opposites is too superficial. A couple who looks very different from each other or grew up in different cultures may be more alike than a couple who looks like they could be related. What makes a couple compatible is not how they look next to each other, but how well their values align.

Staying true to your values is crucial for you to feel happy and in balance in life—and in love. If you value taking risks and your partner is threatened by that fact, you'll have tension in your relationship.

When we consider who we want to be with long term, we need to evaluate each person based on how he or she may be as a partner. We should ask ourselves if we can appreciate and celebrate the differences between us, instead of trying to make the other person more like ourselves.

One of my basic relationship principles is that *people want to be challenged—not changed.* The quickest way to disconnect from someone is to step on his or her values and what makes that person inherently unique. That's not to say we can't grow into a better version of ourselves with a good match, but we shouldn't start off by trying to make our "opposite" exactly like us. (I'm not sure about you, but I wouldn't want to date my double. Actually, that would be creepy.)

The bottom line is that opposites attract for a long-term partnership only when they are looking for the same basic things out of life and, ultimately, when they stand for the same deep principles. And in that case, they're not really that opposite.

Do Opposites Attract?

"Opposites attract, and then annoy the f*** out of each other."
—Rochelle

"Paula Abdul and MC Skat Kat sang about that. Pretty sure they're no longer together." —Kevin

"If you mean opposites who attract and are good together, I think they're opposite in more secondary areas, like musical tastes and even dispositions, but alike in fundamental areas, like life goals and family values." —Kristine

"Opposites attract. I am an extrovert, and my hubby is an introvert. Together, we balance each other. The only place I cannot envision opposites attracting is one where strong religious beliefs are concerned." —Tara

"They attract and then, much like combustible atoms, explode."
—Lisa

"Any two people can find areas that they feel they are 'opposite' in. However, without similar beliefs and similar interests, it's going to create drama." —Corie

"'Opposites attract'—that's the shit you say when you obviously see differences but still want some of that ass...." —James

EXPECT A SATURDAY NIGHT DATE

ANDREA

Unless the guy you're seeing is on special assignment every weekend, I would question why he never makes time to hang out Friday or Saturday night. Traditionally, weekend nights are "date nights," because we can hang out without worrying about work the next morning. A fabulous Saturday night date can extend into a Sunday morning brunch plan. To be frank, this may be one reason he's avoiding booking a date with you on a weekend—he may not want an extended date. But if he can't even make that time commitment, he may not be ready for any kind of significant commitment with you. You're not paranoid to question where you stand.

In the words of my friend John, "If I'm not sure I'm really into a girl, I don't want to give her my Saturday night. I'd rather head out with friends to meet new girls or take someone out that I really like." Ouch. I do believe that men communicate through actions more than words, so notice what kind of effort he's putting in to see you and spend time together. If you feel like it's few and far between and he's generally available only at really unsexy times, like Monday from 5:30-6:30 p.m. or Sunday at 3 p.m., consider moving on or at least adding more men to your rotation who would love to take you out on Saturday night.

JEFF

If he never wants to go out with you on Saturday, should you ditch the dude?

Well, yes. Basically.

Actions speak louder than words. And while I reject the hard-line zealotry of "He's just not that into you" (see pages 159–163), if the guy's a ghost on the weekends, if he never wants you to hang with his friends, or if he never suggests that you meet his family, well, as John Adams said, "Facts are stubborn things."

The key is looking at the broader context of his behavior. The guy (or woman) shouldn't be raked over the coals for one specific transgression. Maybe you've been dating for three months, his mom's in town, and he doesn't suggest you meet her: bad sign. Then again, what if this same guy wants to travel with you, spends every weekend with you, and insists that you join his buddies for Thursday Night Trivia? Okay, so he's skittish on the parent thing—a lot of people are—but he's making a solid effort to involve you in his life.

Same thing goes for never wanting to see you on Saturday, or never wanting to hang out with your friends, or Bad Boyfriend Behavior fill-in-the-blank. In isolation, any one of these shouldn't be a deal breaker. A pattern of poor behavior, on the other hand…

If he's coming up empty in multiple categories, call him on it. If I were in the bad boyfriend's shoes, this is the most useful thing a woman could say to me: "Hey, I'm not angry, and I don't think you have an *obligation* to do any of these things, but if we're going to be in each other's lives—if we're in a relationship—it hurts me that you don't X, Y, or Z."

I'm not just making these words up; a woman I was dating gave me that speech. She was right. I had been unwittingly wasting her time. When she called me on it, we broke up...and she prevented herself from wasting any more time with Dead-End Jeff.

Chapter 7

SEEING SOMEONE

The awesome-but-awkward phase when you've been on a few dates and you're not sure if it's monogamous, about to be monogamous, or flingy. And when it gets more serious? The rules haven't vanished just because you're in a relationship. Oh no. They're still here to scare you and make you second-guess.

- By now, you should have met his friends and family
- You can't change him
- If they don't approve, dump him
- Spend most of your time together
- Never say "I love you" first

BY NOW, YOU SHOULD HAVE MET HIS FRIENDS AND FAMILY

JEFF

I did a very mean thing. Several years ago I met a girl at a bar, we hit it off, we hooked up, and then we went out several times. I liked her. We dated for over a month and things were going well, but I couldn't figure out if I liked her or if I *liked* her.

So I thought, *Why not outsource the problem? I'll let my friends decide.* If Apple can outsource their production to China, why couldn't I outsource romance?

"Are you free next weekend?" I asked her.

"Yeah. What's up?" she said.

"No big deal. Just a picnic … with a few of my friends," I said.

Okay, this picnic didn't involve just "some" of my friends; it involved almost all my friends in New York. And okay, so the picnic was part of a wedding weekend. I viewed it as an audition, of sorts. I was curious to see how she'd interact with my friends. Would they approve?

It gets worse. Before the picnic I actually told my crew, "Guys, I'm on the fence on whether I like this girl. It's fifty-fifty, so it's up to you to decide. The ball's in your court. Totally your call. I'm good either way."

At the picnic I introduced her to everyone, we all played Frisbee, and I kept asking my friends, "So whaddya think?" As we sat down on the blanket to drink wine, a few of my friends playfully tossed a softball back and forth, and when she didn't even make an effort to catch the ball, I thought, *Ooooh, minus five points*.

In hindsight my behavior was despicable. The motivation for my invite wasn't "Hey, you mean so much to me, I want to move our relationship forward." The motivation was "I can go either way on this, and maybe if I see you interact with my friends, I'll have clarity."

It was a shady move, and it came at a shady time of my life. This shady time is also known as "my twenties."

Why is this relevant? There are two takeaways:

First, even in this absolute worst-case scenario, I still viewed her as "girlfriend potential" and I wanted to see if we'd click. If I had seen her only as a fling, I never would have bothered. If a guy thinks the relationship is serious, or has the chance to become serious, at some point, he will want you to meet his friends and family. (Even if he's being a dick.) If he's always making excuses, well, "if it talks like a douche and walks like a douche..."

The second, more important takeaway: the fact that I felt I *needed* my friends' approval should have told me everything I needed to know. You can't "outsource" the decision of whether you like someone. And since this issue, like most issues, is gender neutral, you could easily be in the same boat. It's one thing to have anxiety about your friends meeting the person you're dating—that's natural. But if you need their validation? If you're withholding judgment on the guy until your friends weigh in? Then you've already made your judgment.

Q: Does the seven-year itch exist?

ANDREA

The seven-year itch is a myth. It takes some of us only a few years to get restless in a relationship, and I'm sure there are couples who have been together for decades who never get itchy (though I wouldn't really believe them).

I'm a firm believer that our expectations influence our happiness. If we expect all-consuming, passionate love over the course of many years with our partner, we may worry each time the idea of a nap sounds more appealing than the thought of nooky. By the same token, if we expect that the passion must die in our long-term relationship, we may not even try to create the intimate, romantic, or sexy connection we're craving.

Our brains are wired to reward us for finding and feeling love. When we first feel romantic love, we're infected with a powerful love cocktail full of neurotransmitters, such as dopamine, which makes us feel giddy, elated, and blissful. During this first love stage, thought to last from one to three years (eighteen months on average, and three years if we're really lucky), nothing seems more important or more appealing than being with our mate.

But none of us would be productive members of society if we were consumed by the feelings of love and passion all day, so after lusty love stage one, we settle into a much more predictable state. (We also wouldn't raise our kids very well if we stayed drugged by love, so kudos to Mother Nature for thinking this through.) We enter what love doctor Helen Fisher calls "the attachment stage" and feel comforted by and comfortable with our mate. We no longer expect—or necessarily want—to have marathon make-out sessions with our partner.

Just because our brain's chemistry returns to normal after the first few months or years of romantic love, it doesn't mean that the spark has to die. (This was really important for me, the commitment-phobe, to realize.) A romantic relationship can have consistency and novelty. These things are not mutually exclusive. But they do take work.

Part of the work of a long-term relationship is keeping the play alive. By introducing novel experiences on a regular basis, by keeping some mystery alive in your long-term relationship (which may include . . . ahem . . . keeping your bathroom door closed), and by making an effort to stay connected in and outside the bedroom, you can trick your brain into thinking that the love is new. (I'm a little biased, as I wrote an entire book about this!) Some of the same ingredients that were present when you first started dating and falling in love will return temporarily. This has been backed up by science. Psychologist Daniel O'Leary of Stony Brook University scanned the brains of couples who had been together for a few decades and reported still being "very intensely" in love. When these couples talked about their partners, their brains mirrored those of individuals in the early stages of love.

(continued)

Stability and passion can coexist in your relationship. Don't avoid long-term love because you're convinced that the spark has to die and you'll get a serious case of the blahs. There will be days when you will be bored and a little itchy . . . but there will be days when you'll look at your partner and he'll be the only one you'll want to scratch that itch.

JEFF
Ask me again in seven years.

When a guy is excited to be with you, he will make sure to introduce you to his friends and family for three reasons: 1) to show you off, 2) to get their opinion, 3) to merge all the people who are important to him so that they can form relationships of their own.

A woman in one of my recent relationship workshops asked me if she should be concerned that after a year and a half with her boyfriend, she hadn't met any members of his family. She explained, "He's very close with them, but they live in Chicago, so maybe that's why we've never met...." I could tell she didn't believe that theory. A moment later she added, "He has a sister who lives near me in the city. Is it strange I haven't met her, either?"

I think we often ask questions that we know the answers to, but we would prefer that someone else offer an explanation. This woman was asking me her question in the context of wanting to know if her partner was ready for marriage. Not only did I not think he was ready to wed, but I didn't even think he was ready to be her boyfriend.

The length of time you date someone does not determine his level of commitment, but when monogamy is involved, it's a fair expectation to meet people close to your partner. If you're a priority and his relationships are a priority, he'll want to make the connection.

Unless all his family and friends reside in Antarctica (in which case you should know—people don't actually live there—he's lying!), or unless he doesn't have a relationship with them (which may raise other questions for you), there will be an opportunity to meet at least a few of his loved ones in some corner of the world. If you don't, the harsh reality is that you probably aren't a great priority in his life.

YOU CAN'T CHANGE HIM

ANDREA

One of my favorite relationship jokes (yes, I have favorite relationship jokes) stars a married couple who have been together for many years. The husband complains, "She changed!" and the wife complains, "He didn't change!"

In my years of relationship coaching I've often heard the same complaints. One woman I worked with, a mother in her late 30s, realized that she was complaining about the very same features that had attracted her to her husband in the first place. When she recognized this, she felt duped by her happy love hormones that had made her fall for her spouse years before.

The reality is that the qualities that attract you to someone often repel you (or concern you) later. If you loved that your boyfriend was driven and hardworking, you may later be annoyed that he prioritizes work too much and comes home late. If you were drawn to his spontaneous spirit, you may complain that you can't pin him down to make plans.

On the other hand, there are a number of women out there who actually like to date fixer-uppers—men who they believe will be better after they've administered a makeover. It's one thing to give a guy a nice fashion do over. (As my friend Michael says, "There comes a point in every relationship—or at least in mine—when the woman will attempt to improve her man's appearance.... In fairness, there usually is room for improvement. Guys generally don't concern themselves with presentation to the extent that women do, so some intervention is often warranted...and even secretly welcome.") But trying to change his personality, his values, and his life goals may lead to disappointment on your end and resentment on his.

A good woman can make a good man better (and the reverse is certainly true, too), but the change and growth should be organic and should be initiated by your partner because he wants to change—not because he feels pressured to live up to a standard set by you...or by your parents. So I agree with the rule that you can't change him. (Nor can he change you.)

As I mentioned earlier, one of my basic relationship principles is that people want to be challenged, not changed. The man you're with doesn't want to be with a doormat (I certainly hope not) and likes you because you're someone who inspires and motivates him to be a better version of himself. And that's how you'll know if you're on the right path: you're challenging him not because you really want to change him, but because you want to help him reach his potential. This is motivated and driven by him, but supported and encouraged by you.

Ask yourself: Are you pushing your man (in a gentle and helpful way, of course!) because you see there's something he deeply values that he's not achieving? Are you challenging him to approach something he cares about with a different perspective so that he can achieve *his* goals? Or are you hoping that with enough of your input and direction, he'll adopt your values?

In relationships we often do things for each other that we don't always feel like doing, just because we know it will make our partner happy. We meet halfway. Relationships are full of compromise—that's what a partnership is all about, after all. Just make sure your partner isn't showing up completely on your side of every issue, plan and approach, and compromising who he is, and you'll both be better off.

JEFF

You can change a sulky child. You can change a puppy who still pees on the carpet. But you can't change the guy you're dating, any more than he can change you.

One of my favorite Andrea-isms is "Don't date the potential. Date the person." She's right. We're deluding ourselves when we think, *I like this 90 percent of this personality—he's funny, he's tall, and he plays the guitar—but I don't like the other 10 percent. He hates commitment. I'll change that.*

Whatever you don't like about the person is probably there for good. The dude's a fully formed man. He's done. Maybe he's a constant cheater? Maybe he's had five wives? Maybe he's cold and never opens up? What you see is what you get.

I've been on the flip side of this. I had an eight-year stretch without any relationships longer than two months. Fling after fling after fling. (Red flag?) I was always upfront about my issues and limitations, but there were still women who thought, *He hasn't been serious with anyone before, but I'm different. This is different.*

To some extent they were right. These women were different, I respected them, I felt lucky to be with them, and I knew it should be more than a fling. I knew I should make it work.

I knew it…but I didn't feel it. There was nothing they could say or do that could change that, change me. My issues were too deeply entrenched. I was dug in.

So the next time you see a guy who looks like damaged goods? He probably is.

IF THEY DON'T APPROVE, DUMP HIM

Let's be clear about one thing. If your friends don't like him, it's very, very rare that they'll actually say something. It's usually more subtle. You have to pick up on the cues:

They say he's "nice"
Ouch. This is code for, "He's more boring than my old calculus professor. And uglier, too. Don't get me wrong! He's nice. Super nice. He might be a good backup option for you someday…if your face is burned in a tragic explosion." (Aside: This is reason #1,386 that I love my mother. I once told her a woman I was dating was nice, and she said, "Oh, sweetie. I'm sorry. You must not really like her.")
They never suggest that you bring him as a +1
If, after they've met, your girlfriends never suggest that he tags along? They sort of think he sucks.

They never ask questions about him

They want him out of sight, out of mind. They're convinced that he'll be a very short-term mistake — like drinking Red Bull and vodka — from which you will soon recover. They have no interest in learning more about him, because the less *real* he is, the better.

They ask snarky, loaded questions

"So he sells shoes for a living, huh?"

"Oh. Good for him. Does he *like* living with his parents?"

"Does he ... um ... always drink this much?"

How much stock should you place in all this? It's probably a moot point. Chances are, if you really like the guy, you're going to keep dating him no matter what you hear from the peanut gallery. No one ever says, "You know this guy was amaaazzzing! But my parents didn't like him, so we broke up." That had more currency two hundred years ago, back when we had a rigid class structure, arranged marriages, and scurvy.

So let's be more realistic. Even though you won't act on their negativity, is it a red flag? *Should* you give their reactions any credence? On the one hand, obviously, you know him better than they do, and there's probably a side of him that they haven't seen. Maybe he's nervous and appears boring in public, but with you he's charming and dynamic. Maybe he treats you like a princess, but they caught him on a bad day. Maybe they're just jealous and mean-spirited.

But I have a slightly different theory. When you're around your good friends, this is you at your most *you*. We all subtly shade our personalities in different contexts—there's the work you, the visiting grandma you, the first-date you—but you hanging with your friends is the most unfettered, unfiltered, unaltered sense of you in your basic state of identity. So your friends know it pretty well. And your friends are generally a good reflection of your core personality, too. So if they, en masse, really hate the guy you're dating? I'm not saying it's the kiss of death. I'm not saying you should immediately dump the guy (you won't).

But there's a good chance that, six months from now, they'll be fighting the urge to say "I told you so."

ANDREA

What would you do if you were seeing someone but knew that your friends and family didn't approve of him? It's tough to reconcile your instinct that someone is right for you with your family's and friends' feelings that he may not be a good match. But sometimes friends and family see something that we simply can't see—or don't want to—in our relationship. (Love goggles don't always give us the full picture.)

Years ago a friend of mine was really into a guy that nobody approved of. We didn't tell her the guy she was seeing was bad news because we didn't want her to be happy; we mentioned it because we saw that he didn't bring out her best (read "she turned crazy").

This guy would go to "work" at ten in the evening, which would've been okay if he weren't a public school teacher. He would call her at odd hours and cancel plans at the last minute. In this case, my friend's feelings for her boyfriend got in the way of her better judgment that the dude probably had a secret life.

However, sometimes family members and friends impose their opinion that someone isn't good enough for their loved one for no other reason than the fact that the guy doesn't reflect *their* values. This scenario has happened to a number of the people I know. They're excited about a new boyfriend who treats them well, but are told by others that they could "do better." This feedback leaves them feeling anxious and confused. And that's the funny thing about seeking other people's opinions and approval when it comes to who you choose to date or marry (or how you live your life, for that matter): replacing someone else's values or "shoulds" with your own wants is a recipe for dissatisfaction.

Think of the countless friends and family members who seem happy with a guy who you would never choose to date, even if you were given a fine incentive package. Just because you wouldn't be with wisecracking Joe doesn't mean your friend doesn't love him and his jokes.

Of course, you want your loved ones to love the person you're with, but dating someone they want you to be with versus someone you really want to be with will generally result in a relationship full of resentment—not just between you and your boyfriend, but also between you and your family.

If judgy friends or family members are telling you qualities about your mate that you know have no basis in truth, challenge them and challenge yourself to find evidence to the contrary. Do they think he's selfish? Do you have evidence to support or refute that claim? If you don't, consider the fact that people who love you may be seeing something you are missing. If you do, consider finding a way to silence their judgments, and create boundaries so you can enjoy a relationship that feels right to you.

> Q: How do you bring up talking about the future?

JEFF

Bring it up on the first date. That's the best way to do it—you get all your issues on the table from Day One. Before you finish your first round of drinks, you should decide if your wedding should have a band or a DJ, when you want to buy a house, and the names of your first two children.

More seriously, this is the kind of thing that you just do whenever it feels natural. There's no set timetable. There's no right or wrong phrasing. Even if the conversation is awkward? It's worth it. It's better to have short-term awkwardness than long-term conflicts.

(continued)

If you're having anxiety about the future, then you should talk about the future. I've written about how men, as a gender, are uncomfortable talking about emotions. And yes, this is true, and yes, this is even supported by neuroscience and cultural studies, and yes, these conversations might cause heartburn. So there's a good chance the man doesn't want to talk about it. My response: tough shit, he has to. Don't let him stonewall you. Most guys don't really want to talk about emotional issues, but we don't really *want* to go to the dentist, either, but we do it for our long-term health.

So if something's bothering you? Don't wait for the problem to turn into a root canal.

SPEND MOST OF YOUR TIME TOGETHER

ANDREA

When we're first falling in love, it's like our brains are on drugs: there's little other than spending time with our partners that gets us high. The parts of the brain that are lit up by romantic love (including the ventral tegmental area, which is connected to pleasure) are also activated when someone shoots up.

In addition to acting high on love, our brains display the patterns of people with obsessive-compulsive disorder (OCD) when we first fall for someone. The neurological pathways in our brains are intensely focused on the object of our desire—so much so, that we want to overdose on the euphoric feelings. After spending a whole day together, we wake up thinking about our love and crave more connection. Not taking a hit of our new beau during this stage of our relationship may even cause us to experience withdrawal. Literally. (By the way, we also experience this kind of withdrawal during a breakup, which is a cruel trick our brains play on us to keep us together.)

So essentially, our brains work hard to keep us with our mate so we can preserve the human race (no pressure). However, this intoxicating "I must be with my honey at all times!" feeling will dissipate as the chemistry of our brains changes and returns to a more normal and balanced state. That's a good thing. After the love rush wears off, after about eighteen months on average, we may even come to a point where we crave a little space from each other. . . .

Think of it this way: A kid cries when her mom leaves her side, but later, as a teenager, she rolls her eyes when her mom *won't* leave her side. She still loves her mom, of course, but craves a little independence. As a relationship matures, the same thing may happen. At this point, you may want occasional time apart from your boyfriend. (Gasp! He may too!) This isn't a sign that something is wrong. In fact, it may show how comfortable you are with each other and prove that you've developed a healthy level of trust.

It's always surprised me to see people who are threatened that their partners have outlets outside of the relationship, since they would never have been attracted to their partner in the first place if he/she didn't have a life. The fact that your partner has interests, outlets, and a social life is a great thing.

Don't believe the hype that happy couples do (and should do) everything together. The happiest couples that I've interviewed report that their relationship works because they have a happy and dynamic life together and an active and interesting life apart. They prioritize their relationship, but they also find time to prioritize their interests outside of it.

The average couple spends 2.5 hours a day together, including weekends, according to a survey by the Office for National Statistics.

Is that too little? Too much?

If you poll one hundred marriage counselors, all one hundred will tell you that every relationship needs space. This is a cliché, but it's true. It's good to have your own interests, your own friends, your own you. This helps recharge your batteries. "Sharing your life" does not mean "sharing every second."

Besides, it's not the quantity of time together that counts; it's the quality. According to that same survey, on average, a full third of a couple's time is spent watching TV. Yikes. Are you connecting with your partner, or are you in the same room while you each play Angry Birds? As psychologist Sherry Turkle writes in the *New York Times*, "We are tempted to think that our little 'sips' of online connection add up to a big gulp of real conversation. But they don't. Email, Twitter, Facebook, all of these have their places in politics, commerce, romance and friendship. But no matter how valuable, they do not substitute for conversation."

It's better to carve out *some* time that allows for these big gulps of real conversation. That means no TV, no checking email, no multitasking. When I was a kid, my parents had a strict "no answering phone calls and no TV" policy at the dinner table. Us kids hated this, but we learned to respect honest-to-God conversations. Quality over quantity.

NEVER SAY "I LOVE YOU" FIRST

JEFF

I'll be the first to admit it: me writing this essay is like the captain of the Titanic writing "How to Stay Safe at Sea," or Mike Tyson writing "Ten Tips for Keeping Your Cool," or Snooki writing "The Dos and Don'ts of Neurosurgery." I've failed at love again and again.

I've taken love for granted. I've lost love. Out-of-my-league women have loved me, and I didn't know how to reciprocate.

I've said "I love you" when I thought I meant it—I've never been disingenuous—but I've never really had *that feeling*.

So what does this have to do with a book on dating rules? Nothing and everything. I'd like to think that the concept of love still has an element of magic, and that magic can't be captured, codified, quantified, or carved up into a pithy rule. Love doesn't fit in a box. I reject any guideline like "Wait two months to say 'I love you!'" or "Never be the first to say 'I love you.'"

Sure, anyone older than fourteen knows that you shouldn't tell someone "I love you" on the first date. But what about after two weeks? A month? Six months? A year? Who knows? It's impossible to give an answer that's one size fits all. The bottom line is as simple as this: if you love someone, tell them.

What about the old cliché that men hate saying "I love you" first? As a joke, in my last book I even codified this as a rule: "Maxim of Manhood 21: Use every four-letter word but one." Honestly? Not much truth to this. In a survey conducted by the *Journal of Personality and Social Psychology*, over 60 percent of the men reported that they said "I love you" first. (The survey only had a sample size of one hundred MIT students, but still.)

What should you do if you're dating someone (like me) who struggles to say "I love you," and you've been dating for months and months—maybe a year—and he still hasn't said it, and you still haven't said it, but you know that you love him? It's possible that he's just gun-shy. It's also possible that he doesn't love you.

Life is short. And the worst part is the nagging uncertainty, the doubts, the *not knowing*. Be the strong one and tell him you love him. If he doesn't respond in kind...well...now you know. It doesn't really matter who says it first. Pride goes only so far, and romance shouldn't be a game of chicken.

ANDREA

In one of my favorite films, *Annie Hall*, Alvy tells Annie, "*Love* is, is too weak a word for what I feel. I *lurve* you, you know. I loave you. I luff you.... Two *f*'s, yes, I have to invent. Of course I—I do. Don't you think I do?"

I love how awkward, vulnerable, endearing, and romantic Alvy is in that moment. And I love how much truth that line has for so many of us when we experience romantic love. *Love* does seem like too small a word to capture the feelings associated with it. When you first feel romantic love for someone, you don't want to say it. You want to scream it, be consumed by it, and be enveloped by it. (Melodramatic, aren't we?)

The initial "I love you" in a relationship is often exciting and nerve-racking. Few people want to be the one to say it first, but sometimes it's difficult to contain.

I remember an ex whispered it in my ear one night while we were sleeping. I could tell the next morning that he hoped I'd think his "I love you" was a dream. For another month, we both pretended he didn't say it, until he said it again with the strange preface, "I know you aren't feeling the feelings I'm feeling now ... but I still want to tell you ... I love you." I responded as automatically as you would to the question "How are you?" with a quick "Fine!" even if you weren't. I promptly said, "Me too!" quite unconvincingly. He looked me in the eyes and said, "I know you don't. And that's okay. I just wanted to let you know that I do...."

In that moment, I thought of the age-old grandma advice, "Marry a man who loves you more than you love him." Whether or not you agree with that tip, I do think it's good to marry a man who loves you. A lot. However, the hope is that you're also excited to be with him, and that you share his feelings and reciprocate instead of cringe when he tells you how he feels. (Ultimately, I never said it back and we broke up a few months later.)

It's a basic human need for all of us to be loved, acknowledged, and appreciated for who we are. It doesn't necessarily make the world go round, but it certainly feels good. The downside is that feeling intense romantic love for someone can, paradoxically, *distract* you from the right match.

Love does not a relationship make! We need to be in like with our partners and like ourselves around them. Like is underrated but can help us see more clearly if someone is good for us. How many times have you heard a woman say, "He doesn't treat me right, but I *love* him" as justification for staying together?

Focus on finding someone you not only love in the grand moments but also like and trust in the quiet moments. And in that case, it doesn't really matter who says "I love you" first.

Saying I Love You

"Lisa was riding her bike and a cab nearly hit her, and instead of shouting 'Be careful,' I accidentally shouted 'I love you.' People clapped. It was pretty embarrassing…but it worked!" —Vicki

"I once dated a guy who had a very hard time expressing his feelings. When he finally told me he loved me (after we'd been seeing each other for over a year), it came out like this: 'Okay, fine. I love you. But I love a lot of things, like ice cream.' Needless to say, it didn't work out." —Kara

"In the middle of a fight, he said, 'Well, damn it, I love you, even when you're being like this.' It ended the fight and I started laughing." —Taylor

"He said 'I love you' the first time on Skype and told me that he had a dream that he told me." —Michelle

"First date. First words out of his mouth, 'My ex-wife wants to have another baby. Do you want babies?' He said it was the dumbest thing to say, but he knew I was The One and that's what came out." —Cole

"Oh, man. We were drunk, on our third date, and as we were falling asleep together, he said he loved me. I was so shocked and horrified, I pretended I was already asleep. Then he said it again, louder this time. I shut my eyes and wished the moment would pass. Wished so hard that I farted, loud and juicy, right on his leg. That taught him—he never said it again!" —Tara

Chapter 8
BREAKING UP

Let's be honest. The majority of relationships don't last. And even the process of breaking up is riddled with rules. Given that harsh reality, we'll examine the following:

- You need a rebound
- Don't try to be friends with your ex
- Take a break

> ## Q: Are you ready for a breakup?

ANDREA

As you know, I don't have many rules when it comes to dating, but one thing I'm quite certain about is the fact that when you're with a good match and ready for a serious commitment, the thought of being with him doesn't torture you.

I've been in relationships in which I practically had to conduct market research to determine whether or not we should stay together. I wouldn't confide only in my friends for their opinions. I'd also find myself opening up to virtual strangers at parties to get them to weigh in on my situation, which, by the way, generally made me feel worse. This crazy gal move should've been a sign that I wasn't ready to get more serious with the person I was dating, but I didn't see it at the time.

When you're ready to move forward and commit to something more long term with your boyfriend, I believe it will be a feeling, not a thought. You won't have to add up criteria on paper or conduct polls on the street, and you won't lie awake at night, feeling unbelievably anxious, confused, and unclear. You won't be in your head at every moment, trying to weigh the pros and cons of the relationship. That's not to say that you won't ever feel discomfort as you get closer to someone. It's scary to open yourself up to a person you love and let him into your life in a deep and intimate way. You may experience internal and external resistance when you do this, just as you would with anything that pushes you outside of your comfort zone.

The way you'll know the difference between "I'm acting crazy because I secretly don't think this is my match" versus "I'm acting crazy because it's scary to feel so vulnerable with someone I care about" is to gauge how you feel when you're actually *with* the person in question. When you're together, are you in your head, looking at him critically, weighing everything he says or does against the question "Can I really be with this person?"

Do you find yourself finding faults with most things he does or shrieking at his idiosyncrasies? (A good friend's mother once told me, "If you don't like the way he eats his cereal, he's not for you.")

Or do you find that when you're with him, your mind chatter is quieted? Do you feel comfortable, happy, excited, and generally present when you're together?

As you know, my litmus test to determine whether or not something is an authentic decision in your life is to ask yourself, "Is this a 'should' or a 'want'?" Notice whose voice pops into your head when you consider this question.

One of the guys I dated (and was constantly confused about) would've been perfect...for my father. He had everything my father was looking for in a mate (well, not *everything*), but he didn't really have the qualities I wanted in a long-term partner. On the other hand, my husband was someone I wasn't sure I *should* be with, but few people could convince me that I didn't *want* to be there, because I knew how I felt when I was around him.

(continued)

As a former commitment-phobic, confused gal, I can assure you that you will feel clarity as you quiet your mind chatter. As you learn to listen to your heart and gut and consider practical matters of how you can build a life with someone, you'll have your answer to whether you want to stay in the relationship or move on.

JEFF

Probably. You should dump the guy. (Kidding!) Relationships are never simple. Context is everything, so I won't presume to give you any global advice, but I can suggest some questions.

There's no scorecard for this little quiz. There's no Myers-Briggs-esque "Add up the scores in column one, subtract the scores from column two, and if the final number is greater than thirteen, throw his ass to the curb."

Ten Questions

1. **Your phone rings. The caller ID says that it's him. Is your first reaction excited or bummed?** This is a great barometer. It's an unfiltered, unprocessed, direct insight into how you really feel about the guy. This doesn't mean, necessarily, that you need to visualize rainbows every time he calls, but if your default reaction is anxiety, well, that means something.

2. **He's out of town for two weeks. Quick gut reaction: is this good news or bad news?** If this is good news, you're in luck, because I have some ever better news. Once you break up, he'll be out of your life forever.

3. **Does this person make you happy?** If you have to think more than five seconds, then the answer is no. And if that's the case, why do you want to be with someone who doesn't make you happy? End it.

4. **Have you given it a real shot?** This doesn't mean that you need to give every Y chromosome in your zip code a "real shot." But let's say you're into a guy, and then things get more serious, and then, for no real reason, you freak out. Maybe you're afraid of commitment (been there, done that), maybe you think you're just "not a relationship person" (also been there), or maybe you're playing the "It's not you, it's me" card (yep, been there, too). You're entitled to do whatever you want, but before you chuck the relationship, think about whether the problem is the guy, or your mindset. And maybe your mindset is *I must be single*. If that's what you want, that's fine, too.

5. **Does he treat you with respect?** See number 3. If the answer is anything close to no, walk away this second.

6. **Do you still like kissing him?** Physical attraction matters. This doesn't mean he needs to be a bronze god that could double as July on a sexy firemen calendar, but generally speaking, does the thought of a make-out session give you the skeevies?

7. **Are you long-term incompatible?** Maybe you've been dating for two years and you've had a good run,

(continued)

but ultimately, he wants kids and you don't, and neither of you will ever budge. Fair enough.

8. **Are you really long-term incompatible?** That previous scenario (about the kids) is a little extreme. It's usually murkier. Challenge yourself to determine if the issue is truly a deal breaker, or if it's more a preference that's open to compromise, like, say, whether your kids would go to public or private school.

9. **Do you love him?** This is sort of a trick question, as "Do you love him?" is less helpful than you think. The question is so overly broad and tough to answer; it's almost like when someone asks, "What should I do?" and you respond, "Well, what do you *think* you should do?" Not terribly constructive. That said, if you don't love him after a year, you're probably not going to start.

10. **What are your options if you break up?** This is absolutely a trick question. When you're deciding if you should stay with someone, *your other options do not matter.* They're irrelevant. Some people fall into the trap of "Well, I'm not sure how happy I am with Judy, but hell, I'm 39 years old and the dating scene in Montana sucks, so screw it. I'll just ride it out with Judy." You deserve to be with your partner regardless of options B, C, or Z. Never date a consolation prize. Disclaimer: I've never dated in Montana, so that might be an exception. Apologies to all Montanans who are dating a woman named Judy.

Confessions of a Bad Breaker-Upper

JEFF

I've been a bad breaker-upper too many times to count.
Out of respect for my exes I won't get into specifics, but
just to shed some light on dumb male behavior, here's my
thought process:

What I did

Got a girl's number at a bar. Then never called.

What I was thinking

This happened a lot. This is how it usually played out:
I'm flirting with a girl at Dolan's Tavern—hey, we're at
a bar, she's cute, so why not?—and then, at the end of the
conversation, it's only natural to swap digits. It'd feel rude
not to ask for her number. Then a couple of days go by
and I'd think, *Hey, maybe I should call Dolan's Tavern
Girl.* But then I'm busy and I forget, and suddenly it's the
following week, and by then I've sort of lost interest. (What
was her name again? She had dark hair, right? Or blond?
Definitely one of the two.)

What I did

Ended things after a promising three months.
With no warning.

What I was thinking

It comes as a bombshell. Our dates are fun, we click, and
everything's all blue skies and cotton candy. Suddenly

bam! I end it with no warning. My thought process? Yes, we have fun together and I'm into her, but my Spidey Sense detects some structural problems in the relationship or, at times, structural problems in me. I've sensed that I'm either (a) not ready for a serious relationship or (b) not ready for a serious relationship with her; and when it's the latter, that's not something you necessarily know on dates one or two. It takes a while to learn this, and that's what dating's all about. And since I'm an outwardly chipper person, things continue to look blue skies and cotton candy, even while I ruminate and doubt. Would it be more healthy, more fair, and more mature to openly communicate these doubts? Of course! But I'm not describing the right way to act or think; I'm describing how I—and a lot of men—actually act and think. (Or how I *acted*, past tense. Most of these are well in the past. I like to think I've grown and learned. Kind of.)

What I did

After we hooked up ... I faded out.

What I was thinking

The rationale: It's never an intentional thing. I'm not stringing her along, thinking, *Okay, I'll go out with her until we hook up, and then once I've gotten the goods, I'll vanish.*

Sometimes I disappear after the first date (when we don't hook up); sometimes I disappear after the fifth date (when we hooked up on the second date); sometimes I disappeared after the first date (when we do hook up). In the past it was rare for me to have a long relationship, so we're probably only going on a few dates no matter what. First-date, second-date, or seventh-date hookup? That's not a deciding factor in whether I stay or go.

This is the critical flaw with the "Oh no, we hooked up and he never wants to go out again, so we shouldn't have hooked up!" mindset. It's misidentifying the root cause. The problem isn't that you hooked up; the problem is that the guy is an asshole.

YOU NEED A REBOUND

ANDREA

When I broke up with my ex of five years, I cried so hard that the skin on my nose started to peel from blowing it so much. And then, after a few sulky weeks, I started dating (way too many) men until I felt exhausted. (Basically, I binged on being single again.) There were times that I felt crazy at the thought of leaving a wonderful man, and times I felt peace and clarity, knowing that I had followed my heart. I often went through this range of emotions in a few short minutes.

There's not one right way to process a breakup, or any life challenge, for that matter. Some people will tell you that you need to go wild and date a lot (have a rebound!), while others will suggest that the best thing you can do to heal your heart is have quiet time alone. You'll have friends and family admit that they never really saw you with your ex, which will make you feel like they were judging your relationship while you were together, and some who will try to convince you (or him) to give it another shot because you're "perfect" for each other. As you process your breakup, people's advice may be both comforting and confusing. After all, it's hard for anyone to tell you how you should feel.

What I learned is that the best thing I could do at the time of my breakup was to follow exactly what felt right for me in each difficult moment. I couldn't predict those moments in advance. I'd break down when I saw a monkey on TV that I knew we'd laugh at together, but I didn't feel sad on Valentine's Day or other holidays we would've shared. There wasn't a right or wrong way for me to process it, as long as I processed it at some point.

Nature plays a cruel trick on us when we've separated from someone we love. Our brains actually want us to stay together and work hard to make that happen. Evolutionary biologist Dr. Helen Fisher conducted a post-breakup experiment a few years ago. She worked with a group of people who had just ended a relationship and reported feeling very in love with their exes. Her team scanned the brains of these participants and found that their brains mirrored those of people who were suffering from cocaine addiction or physical pain. They were literally experiencing withdrawal—scientific evidence of very real heartache.

Dr. Fisher notes that when you're going through a breakup, "you're feeling romantic love, you're in physical pain and you're in a state of constant craving. That's a very bad combination for getting to work on time!"

You may not feel like yourself when you're processing a breakup, and it's normal to feel ... well, not so normal. The important thing is that you give yourself time and space to grieve (or celebrate) so that you'll be ready to date the person who is a better match for you when he comes along.

Other things to keep in mind while you process your breakup:

1. **Look back.** Looking back and replaying what you coulda, woulda, shoulda said or done is not helpful, but there's a lot to learn from relationships that don't work out. Were there signs that you ignored that the relationship wasn't working? What have you learned?

2. **Stay present.** Do you feel like grieving or going out for a fun night on the town? Listen to your gut through the difficult weeks following your split, so your post-breakup feelings don't manifest in messy ways.

3. **Move forward.** Make new relationship resolutions. Who do you want to be, and who do you want to be with in the months and years ahead?

There's only one thing you really need after a breakup: alcohol.

Okay, so maybe we need a little more than that. It also helps to have a distraction, and this distraction can come in the form of a rebound, or a fling, or just harmless flirting. Or maybe it's a distraction that has nothing to do with romance or sex; maybe you want to travel more, work more, Big Sister more.

If your chosen distraction is a rebound? Look, there are always exceptions, but in the shadow of breakup carnage, you're probably not ready for anything serious. And if you think you *are* ready...you're probably not. (Sorry.) We all need some time to process, reflect, grieve, and do what clinical psychologists call "get our shit together."

That doesn't mean you shouldn't do it. It just means you need to have realistic expectations, and it means that you need to be honest about where you're at—and where you're not at—with Rebound Guy.

If you have a rebound, great, but if you don't have one, that's also great. Who cares? The mandate "You need a rebound!" ironically serves only to inject more anxiety into the breakup, as now, in addition to getting over the last boyfriend, you have peer pressure to hook up with someone new.

Besides, what's wrong with doing nothing for a while? What's wrong with enjoying being single? Maybe you want to spend more time with your friends, maybe you want to clear your head in solitude, or maybe you want to finally read *Infinite Jest*. Everyone deals with breakups differently, and there's no one and only right answer, besides tequila.

DON'T TRY TO BE FRIENDS WITH YOUR EX

JEFF

Should you be friends with your ex? Short answer: maybe, but not right away. Longer answer: it depends on four variables:

1. The nature of your friendship pre-dating
2. The size of the emotion gap
3. The acrimony of the breakup
4. The buddy buffer

The nature of the friendship pre-dating
If you were friends before you started dating, then the stakes are higher, you have years of history, you have gobs of mutual friends, and you probably want to keep him in your life. This can be done, but it still takes time.
The size of the emotion gap
The bigger the gap, the tougher it is to be friends. When he's heartbroken and you're meh, you might

think it's easy-breezy to be his pal, but every time he sees you, he chokes back tears like Jason Segel from *Forgetting Sarah Marshall*. A true friendship is possible only when this gap narrows, and that, too, can happen only with time.

The acrimony of the breakup

Pretty straightforward. No breakups are good breakups—even when they're done at the right time for the right reasons, they still suck—but the true soap operas take more time.

The buddy buffer

You need some buffer, some space, and some time to reframe this person before you make them your buddy. Buddies don't see each other naked. Buddies don't spoon. And buddies don't freak out when birthdays approach, wondering what they should get as a gift. If you break up on Tuesday, you simply can't be his buddy on Wednesday. You need that buffer. This buffer—space away from him, time away from him, and less/no communication with him—helps rewire the circuitry of your relationship. Without that buffer, it's easy to think you're just "being friends," while you're actually *acting* like you're still in a relationship, minus the sex. (Examples: still texting all the time, still confiding in him for work advice, still swapping inside jokes.) This just prolongs the inevitable; it keeps both of you from doing the hard work of getting over each other, and it keeps you from opening up to someone new.

So it's absolutely possible to become friends again in the future—I've done it, and I'm glad I have—but you first need space, and that space can take a long, long, long damn time.

ANDREA

There's no good reason to stay in touch with an ex shortly after you've broken up. It may seem extreme, but during the months following a split, not only should you avoid seeing your ex, but you should also cut off all access and communication.

Here's the issue with staying in touch after you've broken up: If you have a bad conversation, you will feel bad (and upset to leave it that way). If you have a good conversation, you will feel bad (and will probably miss him more).

Staying in touch delays your chances of moving on and finding someone who is a better match for you.

You may think that being in regular contact with your ex is not holding you back from moving on, but recognize that no new person you date will compare to the comfort* and connection you have had with your ex.

---

* Comfort is all relative, of course. Just because someone knows you, that doesn't mean you feel at ease with him.

So should you lose touch with all your exes?

The short answer is no. With time and distance, I believe many people can remain friends with their ex-boyfriends. In fact, one of my closest friends is the ex that I lived with for five years in California. But we couldn't get to this place immediately: it took a number of difficult and uncomfortable moments over the year that we lost contact. During the first few months of our split, I had to stop myself from sending a note to him on every holiday that we had previously shared.

After about a year of losing touch, we slowly started finding our way back into each other's in-boxes. By this point, we had both moved on and were dating other people. And that's key. It would've been much harder to be in touch if one of us had moved on and the other was still mourning the relationship.

Interestingly, we both got engaged to other people a few weeks apart from each other (two years almost to the day after our relationship ended), and we shared the happy news with each other. It was a strange call, but I could tell that we were both genuinely happy for the other and wanted to make sure we heard it directly, instead of getting the news from a third party. We had entered a new phase of our relationship, and it felt right. It now seems we were always meant to be friends and not romantic partners.

It's been eight years, and he's one of the first people I call when I visit San Francisco, and we always make time to see each other when I'm in town. (I don't take for granted the fact that both of our spouses are comfortable with our friendship.) My ex and I have a phone date every few months so he can update me about his kids and I can tell him about my life in New York. I cherish our current relationship, and in many ways, I appreciate it more than I did when we lived together and were unclear about what we wanted.

I've set other ex-boyfriends up on dates and yet there are some exes that are no longer in my life . . . and that's okay. They served a purpose at one point, and I'm grateful for our time together, but I don't need to stay connected beyond that.

Recognize why you want to stay in touch with your ex, and make a choice that works for you. Just give yourself time before you reconnect so you can appreciate your new relationship with him, and allow yourself to let someone else—someone who is more suitable—come into your life.

Bad Breakup Etiquette

JEFF

So much depends on context. And sometimes there's no such thing as "bad breakup etiquette." For example, if your boyfriend stole money from your purse, then kicked your dog, then slept with your sister—while you're pregnant—and then, as the coup de grâce, deleted *The Bachelor* from your DVR, well, you're entitled to any amount of revenge. But for the normal, run-of-the-mill breakup? It's best to avoid the following:

Cutting the conversation short

If you're the breaker-upper, you have to respect the breakup-ee's filibuster rights; they're allowed to talk to you as long as they want—an hour, two hours, the entire night—and challenge you with any question. This is your penance. You just plopped their heart in a blender, so it's not, therefore, the coolest thing to add, "And yeah... can we wrap this up? I've got tickets to a 7 p.m. movie."

Opening the vault

When you're a couple, you trust each other, you confide in each other, and you tell secrets to each other. The vault must stay sealed *even in the event of a breakup.* A promise is a promise. If he told you that his uncle's a cross-dresser, you need to take that secret to the grave. (Note to family: This is not a personal anecdote. None of my uncles are cross-dressers, not that there's anything wrong with that.)

Using them for breakup sex

Breakup sex is fair game under one, and only one, condition: when you're on the exact same emotional footing. In the history of breakups, this has happened exactly fifteen times.

Breaking up with them at your place

Or at the coffee shop, restaurant, or comedy show. It's easiest to do it at their place—if you're kicking them to the curb, the least you can do is minimize their commute.

Trying to win old fights

When it's over it's over, so what's the point of dregging up old arguments, trying to prove a point about why, five months ago, so-and-so didn't want to go to your birthday party? Who cares?

Hooking up with your ex's friend

Yes, you are *legally* allowed to do this, and you're also *legally* allowed to update your Facebook status every day by saying "I'm an asshole!" Both have the same effect.

Being wishy-washy

If you're ready to end things? Then it's time to take bold, clear, decisive action. Any waffling will prolong their emotional crucible. This is different from when you actually are confused and want to have a serious conversation about where the relationship is headed.

Breakup blogging / tweeting

Writing can be therapeutic, and sometimes an angry Alanis Morissette's "You Oughta Know"-esque diatribe can bring you immediate satisfaction. You'll regret it later. Maybe you think your breakup gives you juicy "raw material!" that would make great fodder for your blog, Tumblr or Twitter feed. I've made this mistake, it still sickens me, and I still regret it, which is why I no longer write about breakup details. They're hard enough as it is. Your ex shouldn't have to see a play-by-play.

Breaking up over the phone or by text or email

Fun fact: Dante's *Inferno* originally contained a tenth level of hell, and it was reserved for people who do this.

TAKE A BREAK

> ## ANDREA

Ah, the infamous break. Rachel and Ross argued incessantly about his trysts while the two were "on a break."

It's harder to pull off than it seems.

The rationale:
You love your boyfriend and aren't ready to end the relationship. But you're confused about where your relationship is going. The break will clear your head and give you an opportunity to figure out what you want or need.

The reality:
It's tough to separate from someone you're used to speaking with or seeing every day. You will miss each other and may not know if it's because you're out of touch or because you're meant to be together.

I understand how appealing it can be to have the option to see how you feel or figure out what you should do without closing the door completely, but sometimes you have to close the door to open your mind and find clarity.

And while I'm speaking in analogies, I should add this: sitting on the fence about a decision is a lot less comfortable than jumping off and landing on one side. Sure, the fall may hurt, but sitting there with the spikes up your butt (sorry for the visual) generally hurts more.

When you pick a side—stay together or break up, in this case—you need a little recovery time to dust yourself off, but you'll be more likely to feel empowered and ready for the next chapter.

If you're going to opt for the break, set some ground rules in advance. For instance, I'd recommend *not* dating others during this time, or you're setting yourself up for disappointment and potential confusing or hurtful feelings. You may also decide to delineate other terms, like the next time you'll be in touch.

The reality is that if you've been with your boyfriend for a while, you know him pretty well. What will you really learn about him that you don't already know during your time apart? You may learn that you miss him, but that result would likely happen even if you weren't meant to be. It's unnatural to have a best friend and not be in touch the next day. It hurts.

This is like the band that goes on "hiatus" for three months…then six months…then two years….and then, ten years later, when no one cares, they release *Chinese Democracy*. Don't be the Guns N' Roses of dating: fix it or end it.

"Breaks" never address the underlying problems. Maybe it's your relationship's lack of chemistry, maybe it's poor communication, or maybe it's a love imbalance. Whatever it is, it won't be solved. Instead, one of four things will happen:

Break Scenario 1:
One of you will start dating someone else, which will cause jealousy, resentment, and a sense of betrayal. It doesn't matter if you've agreed upon certain rules and exceptions; emotions trump logic. This situation will gradually deteriorate, and you will eventually break up.

Break Scenario 2:
Maybe your "break" has nothing to do with a desire to see other people, and it's more about a need for space. Fine. But give it enough time and one of you will still flirt with or date someone else, and this situation will gradually deteriorate and you will eventually break up.

Break Scenario 3:
The space feels good . . . to one of you, at least. Given that you're happier—or he's happier—with this newfound space, this situation will gradually deteriorate and you will eventually break up.

Break Scenario 4:
You both will really miss each other and decide to get back together.

Which of these scenarios is the most problematic?

Break Scenario 4.

When you're on a break, it's completely unsurprising that you will miss the person. You dated him for months or maybe years, so he's your best friend and confidant. You gave him the honor of FTT, or "first text treatment"—when something happens that's funny or exciting, he gets the first text. On a break? The FTT is gone; the sex is gone; the warm security blanket is gone.

The tricky part is that, on a break, you miss only the good stuff and you conveniently forget the bad stuff, and the bad stuff isn't going to change. So if the two of you get back together, all you've done is taken issues on the front burner and moved them to the back burner. The break will become a breakup.

There's one exception: when a couple actually *breaks up* and then, after the split, they realize they're meant for each other. Oddly, this seems to have a higher chance of success, as the motivations are more honest. There's no self-deception. Even the classic/clichéd example of "the break," Ross and Rachel, didn't get back together until years after they actually broke up. (And this happened only when the show finally sputtered out and the writers, desperate, needed to force a happy ending.) Somehow that's different from *pretending* you'll stay together on a hiatus . . . and then ending up like Axl Rose and four new bandmates.

Q: Is breakup sex a bad idea?

JEFF

Breakup sex, a bad idea? Why would you think that?

You just had an emotionally draining conversation, every nerve ending is exposed, maybe you said a few nasty things you'll regret, and you're still processing the fact that the most important—or at least the most prominent—person in your life will suddenly vanish. What better time to get even more vulnerable?

And then, after the sex, you have the antithesis of pillow talk: pillow frost. One of you turns away in frosty anger, cold, distant, slowly realizing *that that was the last time,* and now you feel empty. You fumble to find your clothes—no longer comfortable naked—and you wish the lights were dimmer. Do you leave now, or do you spend the night? The former seems cruel; the latter seems inappropriate. Then you laugh to yourself and think, *Inappropriate?* As if anything about the past seven hours has been appropriate.

Maybe that's how it plays out. Or maybe you have sex, and it's amazingly, headboard-rattlingly awesome. The. Best. Sex. Ever. This makes you happy for a minute, and then you realize that it will never, ever happen again. Unless it does. But you don't want that, right? Or do you? Now, again, you're confused.

Or maybe you feel just fine. You're breezy and chipper. Maybe the sex was good and you're good, but your partner looks at you with a sad smile, hoping for more, hoping to see you again, hoping that actions speak louder than words, and hoping that what you just did—lovemaking—is a signal that you still love him, and that you haven't broken up with him, after all. But you don't love him. And you do want to break up with him. So now you have to do it all over again, and you steel yourself for emotionally draining conversation number two.

Other than all that, no, why would it be a bad idea?

ANDREA

It's certainly tempting to have sex with the guy you were once in a long-term relationship with. You know each other's bodies, hot spots, and how to seduce the other. You can dazzle him with your sexual prowess and make him wonder why the relationship ever ended. Breakup sex is a great way to get sexual satisfaction without commitment. Fun for all!

None of this is true, of course.

In most cases, breakup sex leads to a messy and complicated aftermath. Somehow it feels ickier when your ex doesn't call you back after a hot night than when someone, who you don't even know if you like, goes MIA after a date.

If you were the dumper, you may be making it harder for both of you to move on. (You may think it won't affect you to hook up, but if you care anything about your ex, you'll probably feel a little guilty when you realize you're interested in someone else.)

(continued)

You have a history with your ex. He was once the closest person to you—the one you could confide in about anything. After a breakup, he may transform into a guy you hardly recognize or someone you even feel insecure around. Your baggage with your ex may be full of wonderful things, including resentment, unanswered questions, and hurt feelings. Not so fun.

If you want to have ex sex because maybe he'll remember how great you are, you should know that guys have super-ninja memories when it comes to women's bodies and great sex. (Right, Jeff?) He knows you're hot! Keep that image of you in his head rather than the hot mess you may turn into once you start getting attached to him again.

If you want to have fun no-strings sex, there are plenty of good guys out there who would love to rock your world in bed. I'm all for recycling—but not when it comes to ex-boyfriends.

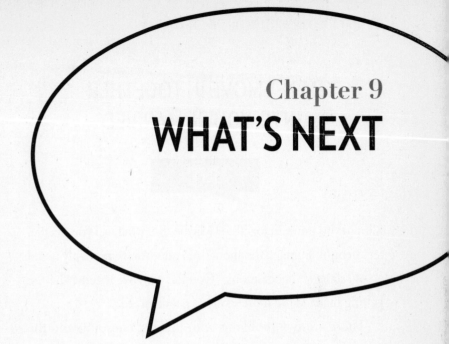

Chapter 9
WHAT'S NEXT

The good news: most of the rules apply to the early phases of dating. Yes, there's an entire industry devoted to relationship and marriage advice...but that's a different book. So we'll just cover a few quickies and get you on your way:

- Don't move in together until you're married
- Give an ultimatum

DON'T MOVE IN TOGETHER UNTIL YOU'RE MARRIED

JEFF

Should you move in together? Maybe. But whatever you decide, let's debunk some myths about this issue. You've probably heard an old statistic that cautions, "Couples who live together before getting married are more likely to get divorced."

There are two problems with this old chestnut, and the first is the fallacy of self-selection. The couples who would never, ever live together before marriage—usually on religious grounds—are often the same couples who would never, ever get divorced, usually also on religious grounds. Conversely, couples who are more likely to shack up, typically, are more open to the idea of divorce if the marriage crumbles. This skews the averages, but it doesn't mean that cohabitation is any more likely to cause divorce. Correlation vs. causation.

The second problem? The research is old, outdated, and now it's just plain wrong. As Hanna Rosin writes in *Slate*, "The 'cohabitation effect' is no longer true. The idea is based on old research from the 1980s. Recently Wendy Manning from the Director of the Center for Family and Demographic Research at Bowling Green State University has analyzed couples married since 1996 and found that the cohabitation effect 'has almost totally faded. We just can't detect it anymore.'"

So whatever you decide, don't let yourself get bullied by people saying, "Oh, if you move in together, you're more likely to get divorced." It's bunk.

As to whether you should do it? Like most things in this book (and life), there's no clear-cut answer. But before you lug your baby grand piano into your guy's living room, keep the following in mind:

Never do it out of necessity
If living with your boyfriend is your only option, you run the risk of feeling trapped. If things go south, you might stay in an unhealthy relationship just because, well, that's where you live. If you find yourself stuck in this scenario, remember that living with a boyfriend is *never* your only option. Never. There's always a way to get by on your own, or with family, or with friends.

Both sides should contribute
This doesn't mean the rent needs to be split fifty-fifty. But if someone's getting a free ride, it tips the scales of power. Resentment can build, bad habits can form, and it deals someone a trump card. Again, it's common for one side to chip in more—no sweat—but 95/5 or 100/0 is combustible math.

An escape hatch doesn't mean you want to escape
Both of you should have an exit strategy, and it's
something you should openly discuss. Scary? Yep,
but moving in together is scary grown-up stuff. Before
you even decide to become roomies, it's smart to have
the conversation that goes, "Okay, so, in the crazy,
nightmarish, almost-impossible-to-fathom, bizarro world
where we break up, who stays in the place, and who
moves out? How do we handle the lease? Furniture? Ice
cube trays?" Establish the ground rules before Day One.
This doesn't mean you want to leave or expect you'll
need to leave, but it gives both of you the confidence
that you're staying in the relationship for the right
reasons, and no, "below market rent!" doesn't count as
a right reason.

ANDREA

Those who propose the theory that you shouldn't move in with
your significant other until marriage believe either that a man is
less likely to put a ring on your finger if you shack up or, more
traditionally, that you'll be living together in sin. For the record,
these are the same people who hate the title of our book.

Hard to believe, but before 1970, cohabitation was actually
illegal in the United States (that's not to say people didn't do it).

It's estimated that today 60 percent of all marriages in the United States start with a period of cohabitation. In 2011 *USA TODAY* headlined a story entitled "Fewer Couples Embrace Marriage; More Live Together."

There are a number of reasons why people choose to live with their partners instead of or before marrying them, including taking advantage of economic incentives, not believing in the institution of marriage, and wanting the convenience that living together affords.

One of the most common reasons I've heard for shacking up is that couples want to test the waters to gauge their long-term compatibility for marriage. These people believe that living with their significant other will help them decide whether or not to make their relationship legally binding. I've even heard people share the "rule" that they would never get married without living with their partner first.

As someone who lived with an ex-boyfriend for five years and has now been living with and married to another man for six, I can tell you that the two experiences are quite different. In a nutshell, here's why: when you get into a disagreement with your live-in boyfriend, or he does something that annoys you, you will use it—and analyze it and obsess about it—to challenge your compatibility as a long-term couple. Your partner will do the same, using your arguments or periods of disconnection as evidence that a marriage with you may not work. You, of course, will also use good moments and happy times shared as justification that you may be compatible. Essentially, you'll both put the other under a magnifying glass on a regular basis.

In marriage, you'll have the same moments of frustration and disconnection that you have when you live with your partner, but the difference is that instead of deciding that the relationship won't work, you'll be more likely to figure out *how* to make it work. You'll learn more about each other and grow from the issues you experience as a team.

All of this is not to say that you won't have real growth in a relationship because you're not married. That's silly. Any relationship you're in will test your patience, your ability to compromise, and your compatibility, but a relationship that's been used to test these things may be setting itself up for an unfair disadvantage.

Of course, you can deduce a lot about living with your partner that would be useful to know before you share a life and potentially raise a family together. You'll see him under stress, you'll be around when he's sick, and you'll experience him when he's tired. You'll also live with him through great times and get a sense of how fun he is to spend time with or how caring he is when you need him.

Here's the thing: you can, and likely will, experience all these things without moving in with your boyfriend. You'll have great nights and stressful days together. You'll have good times and bad. You don't need to move in to see how you'll fare as a couple. After significant time spent together, you should have an idea.

So while I agree with the rule that you shouldn't live together before you get married, it has nothing to do with old-fashioned values and more to do with the fact that relationships don't tend to thrive when they're being tested.

GIVE AN ULTIMATUM

ANDREA

The Millionaire Matchmaker has a rule about engagements: if a guy isn't prepared to put a ring on your finger within the first year of dating, you should be prepared to walk.

There's a slight issue with this rule: you may not want to get married to a guy after dating him for just one year.

There are a number of reasons either or both of you may want to wait before settling down. You may want to finish school, settle into your city, or grow up a little more. You may not even have a reason for wanting to wait more than twelve months to get hitched—and that's okay! Arbitrary timelines for life milestones, such as getting married and having a baby, don't generally help people make authentic decisions. And have I mentioned lately that our brains act wacky during the first year of courtship and romance? Personally, I wouldn't want to make a big investment while my mind wasn't clear of the love drugs. But that's just me.

For all the theories I've heard about the timeline one should stick to for a proposal, I've heard as many (or more) stories of people who rushed down the altar, only to discover later that they weren't really compatible as a couple. To be clear, I'm not saying that those who get engaged after a short time together will have a failed relationship. I know couples who shacked up after just a few months and have been happily married for over thirty years.

There's a happy medium between Judd Apatow's *The Five-Year Engagement* and rushing to the altar, of course. If you're in the situation where you have been dating for a decade and are ready to start the next chapter of your life in wedlock, and your boyfriend would rather talk about anything but your future plans together, it should cause concern. I'd hate for you to be in a position where you felt like you were delaying your needs indefinitely.

In this case, is giving your boyfriend or girlfriend an ultimatum a good idea? Perhaps. By the way, I'd rather refer to this as having a healthy and honest discussion about both of your needs rather than issuing an (cue scary music) "ultimatum." A productive talk about where you stand and what you want out of your relationship is perfectly reasonable after being with your partner for a considerable amount of time. Anyone thinking about getting married should have this talk before moving forward.

Having a "Where do we stand with marriage?" conversation may help you realize that you're on completely different pages (or chapters) in your relationship, and that may propel other big decisions. Or it may spark dialogue and get you closer to your goal.

There are women and men for whom a good old-fashioned ultimatum led them to get married. In fact, a woman I know often brags about how she cornered her husband to get a proposal out of him. She now instructs women, "Men need to be directed! Tell him this is what you need or else!"

I don't know who these men are, but I assume the women who corner men into marriage aren't you. There's a much better and more dignified way to broach an important topic like this with your partner; so find a way to do it to encourage dialogue rather than put him on the defensive. Being pressured into marriage isn't generally the ideal or most romantic way to take that next step.

A breakup can be a unilateral decision, but getting married has to be a mutual one. If you don't hear what you want to hear when you broach the topic, remember that sometimes you have to give yourself what you're waiting for someone else to give you. In this case, it may be a decision.

Is there anything more romantic than an ultimatum? Every good love story ends with the woman putting a gun to her boyfriend's head and whispering, "Be with me, or I'll splatter your brains on the wall."

I don't believe in hard ultimatums, but I do believe in hard communication. At some point, every couple needs to talk about the hard stuff, and if the guy doesn't want to talk about it, tough.

So before saying "Marry me by New Year's Eve … or I'll start dating Paco," let's look at the possible explanations for why the guy is dragging his feet:

**Explanation 1: He doesn't want to marry you …
and never sees that changing.**

Let's get the worst-case scenario out of the way. If he's a lost cause, the sooner you know this, the better, so it makes sense to have a Big Boy talk about where each of you sees the relationship heading. (Note: this makes sense after two years, not two months.) This doesn't mean you need to dump him or threaten to dump him; it just means you say something to the effect of, "Hey, I love you, but here's the thing. I want to raise a family and have kids, and I want to do it with you, but if you don't want to do that, okay, fine, but let me know, so I can move on and find someone who does. Hey, why is everyone shushing me? Okay, we'll finish this conversation after the movie's over."

Explanation 2: He loves you and wants to marry you, but he wants to get other things in his life sorted out first.

The delay might have nothing to do with you personally. I know plenty of guys who had every intention of marrying their girlfriends—and eventually did—but first needed to sort their finances, finish school, or nab that promotion. If that's the case, how will a hard ultimatum accomplish anything, besides draining the proposal of all its romance?

Explanation 3: He loves you and thinks he wants to marry you, but he's skittish and has cold feet.
The most common scenario. The cure for this is the same cure for a hangover, broken heart, or sprained ankle: time. An ultimatum rarely helps, and every guy comes around for different reasons. A good friend of mine, Jimmy, dated his girlfriend for five years and knew he wanted to marry her, but he was happy with the status quo, so he never made the move. Finally, he had his eureka moment: they were buying plane tickets for a trip to Australia fourteen months in advance, and he realized, "Huh, if I'm confident enough that I'll be with her fourteen months from now in the Australian rain forest, I suppose we might as well be married." I doubt those exact words made their way into his proposal, but the point is that, for him, the decision pivoted on something very small. If he has cold feet but deep down he wants to marry you, he'll get there in his own time.

How Did You Know You Were Ready to Get Married?

"The thought of getting married no longer made me feel like puking, as long as it was to him." —Tanya

"When you're dating and asking for advice, people always say 'Just be yourself,' which is, well, hard! When you find the right person, the one you want to spend forever with, you suddenly realize you're mostly yourself when you're with them. I don't mean physically with them, although that's nice too! I mean emotionally…they become a part of you, and I think that's how you know you're ready to take the next step." —Margot

"I looked at her one day and couldn't imagine my life without her, and that's when I knew." —Rob

"When I saw Mathew with my daughter Tamsine, I knew that this was the man I wanted to spend the rest of my life with. That a man could be so genuine and generous with his love to a child that was technically not his own showed me how open he was to love and to loving every piece of me. We now have a total of three children, and I continue to see every day as a blessing." —Christine

"He made me sigh with both pleasure and relief every time he walked in the room. Still does." —Lani

"One day early on in our relationship, we had gone to get some groceries and rent DVDs, and he said, 'We're like a real couple.'

And I said, without holding back, 'You know we're going to get married, right?' And he kind of nodded and we continued on our way. I couldn't believe that those words came out of my mouth! Normally, it would be taboo to talk about marriage so early in a relationship, but this just felt different. There was no game playing, no analyzing every conversation, no pretending to be someone I'm not. It was stress free. And I just knew that he was the One." —Aviva

"I was truly happy and had no feelings of needing something else or someone different." —Tina

"I knew almost instantly. I saw Lisa fussing over a dress while we were getting ready one night and instantly imagined the same scene forty years later. Me in elastic pants and Velcro walking shoes. Lisa in a dress, stockings, pumps, and oversize earrings. It made me feel like I swallowed sunshine." —Vicki

"I once heard it's important to imagine living in a foxhole with the person I loved…without any of the material or superficial additions…and I can't imagine wanting to be with anyone else." —Elana

"She told me (partly kidding)." —Ross

> Q: How do I know if I want
>   to get married?

JEFF

I'm a bit of a paradox. On the one hand, I've never been married. (At least...as of when this book went to press. Maybe this changed after a drunken weekend in Vegas. Who knows? Just in case, to my new wife: I love you, whatever your name is. You're my muse. I dedicate this book to you.) On the other hand, bizzarely, I somehow became an authority on grooms. I'm the founding editor of the groom website ThePlunge. com, and after writing over a hundred articles on weddings, I've found that there are some very good questions to ask before getting engaged...and also plenty of bad reasons to do it. Let's look at both.

Good Questions

Do we see eye to eye on religion? Core values?
This doesn't mean you need to be of the same faith. But have you discussed the extent to which religion will be part of your life and how it will impact the way you'll raise your kids? Speaking of...

Kids? How many?
There are plenty of things you can compromise on.
TV during dinner? Curtains or mini-blinds? This isn't one of them. It's shocking how many spontaneous "I'm in luuuurrrve!" couples take the plunge without even broaching this topic.

Are you acting out of love or lust?

Happily, the two aren't mutually exclusive. But if you met the guy two months ago and you're still in that early, lusty, hormone-crazy phase of the relationship, where, as Andrea has pointed out, your brain is literally on drugs? Not to sound like a parent, but just ask yourself, "What's the downside of waiting?" If you're *meant to be*, then you're meant to be, whether you get married next week or next year. Maybe you. Just. Can't. Wait. Okay, fine, I'll respect that, but this means you need to be extra sure you ask the tough questions.

Do you have the same perspective on money and finances?

Doesn't mean you need to be in lockstep. But if one of you is hell-bent on saving every nickel and one of you likes to rack up credit card debt to buy flat-screens, the issue needs to be squarely addressed.

Do you trust him implicitly?

An underrated question. At ThePlunge.com I had an advice column, and brides wrote me about issues like cheating, jealousy, and the bachelor party. One woman said that her fiancé had "blacked out" at his bachelor party and had woken up naked with his female friend, and should she

(continued)

forgive him? (No.) One groom asked if it's okay to have
oral sex with his female co-worker, because, in his words,
"eating isn't cheating." (My response: just because something
rhymes does not make it true. There's a reason we don't
use the phrase "Schools are for fools.") These are obviously
just the cartoonish extreme examples. But most of the
questions I get from troubled couples are all about trust,
and the lack thereof. If you think you can't really trust him...
then you can't.

Bad Reasons

I want an awesome wedding ceremony!
Do you want a wedding, or do you want a marriage?
Thought experiment: Imagine that you could marry your
boyfriend...but without a ceremony at all, ever. Would
you still want to marry the guy? If the answer is not an
immediate YES, there are some real problems.

Everyone else is getting married.
This has the same logical force as a third grader who
complains, "Mom, but all the cool kids are doing it!"

I'm not getting any younger.
Get married because you've found someone you love
and you want to spend your life with him, not because
he'll do.

It will save us lots of money.
Maybe you're doing it for financial purposes, such as taxes.
But you know what *doesn't* save you money? Divorce papers.

ANDREA

True story: I was called "Runaway Bride" by friends who saw me leave relationships with a string of great men who were ready for marriage.* I was clearly missing the bride gene and came to terms with that fact.

I should note that I also earned the endearing title "31 Flavors" from another guy I dated, because he couldn't imagine I'd ever want to settle down. I'm a person who likes variety in every aspect of my life. The "31 Flavors" nickname was probably appropriate, as I can't even order ice cream without asking the server to combine one flavor with another. Oh, and can I add sprinkles?

So over the years, when people asked me how I'd feel about spending my life with one person, my heart would flutter . . . with palpitations.

You may have gotten by now that my husband, Michael, didn't start out as my "type," so imagine my surprise when I, the gal with eyes bigger than her schedule, started daydreaming about making babies with and baking cakes for this man! I didn't mean to fall in love with him, and that's why I believe it worked.

I was out of my mind—this time in a good way—and listening to my gut feeling that it felt right to be with him. I realized that spending time with him was more fun than not seeing him, and that what I used to think would suffocate me (marriage, gasp!) could actually stretch me, and help me grow into a better version of myself. I started to see that a good relationship could challenge me like nothing else. There was, and still is, a lot to learn. I believe

---

* An ex even told me that he wanted to wish my next boyfriend luck because of my commitment problems.

(continued)

marriage is a choice you have to make every day, and there are many days you won't feel like it, but that doesn't mean it's not rewarding.

I've learned that you can never be perfectly prepared for any life change or big milestone that you haven't experienced before, and most married folks will admit that they still don't know if that someone is the *perfect match* for them. But the happily married ones were willing to take the leap of faith because it somehow felt right.

If you don't know if you're ready to marry your partner, consider this. The real work of a relationship isn't trying to figure out if you should be together. It's *knowing* you're together—and making it work.

CONCLUSION

Okay, so maybe we didn't debunk every rule of dating. And there are plenty of others that we agree with—some no-brainers, some rules so obvious that they can go without saying, like:

- Good relationships have good communication
- Fall in love before getting married
- Don't have sex with your boyfriend's brother

No arguments here. And as we've seen, a lot of the rules have some claims to the truth. While the rules can lead to inauthenticity, insecurity, and eventual incompatibility, it's not that the rules are always bad or always wrong. But for the most part, they're written for those who are less experienced and less savvy. Think about another rule we all heard when we were children: "Never talk to strangers."

A pretty good rule for a 5-year-old, right? But as you get older and have more confidence, you learn that while the original spirit of the rule makes sense—be careful, use your head—it's no longer necessary to follow it literally. It's a rule we outgrow.

And just as we've all outgrown the "Never talk to strangers" rule, most of us have outgrown the dating rules, too. Have confidence in your own ability to make smart choices, evaluate risks, and use your judgment. There's no need to "pretend to be busy." It's not a turnoff that you're "too successful." Don't worry about who's in or out of your league.

Remember that just because the "Never talk to strangers" rule no longer applies, that doesn't mean that the opposite is true, either: "Always talk to strangers." Just because the rule "Never sleep with him on the first date" is outdated doesn't mean the opposite is true: "You should *not* always sleep with him on the first date." It's *okay* to sleep with him on date one, but do it only if you feel safe, comfortable, and protected.

The next time the rules tell you that it's a deal breaker because he texted instead of called, or that you ruined a shot at love because you hooked up too soon, or you hear any other of the dozens of dating rules that we haven't even mentioned, remember that plenty of great relationships started despite (and perhaps because of) breaking these rules. (Don't doubt your instincts in favor of a rule designed by someone who hasn't even met you.)

All that said, we're not nihilists. When we say, "Ignore the rules," we don't mean that people should do whatever they feel like, anytime, anyplace, on the grounds of "Screw it! There are no rules! Mu huha hauh hu!" It doesn't mean we think it's okay to go on a promising first date…and then send the guy twenty-five texts the next day. It doesn't mean we think it's okay to show up to a first date wearing flannel pajamas. And it doesn't mean we think it's okay to sleep with *everyone* on the first date. (There are a lot of creeps out there. Be careful.)

After reading this book, hopefully, you're more aware of all the explicit rules—and implicit rules—that sometimes steer us in the wrong direction. Hopefully, this gives you more confidence to ignore the conventional wisdom, to shake off cynicism, and to listen to your instincts. You know yourself best. And if you've lost faith in the dating process, it may be time to examine your patterns, challenge yourself, figure out what's been working for you and what's *not* been working, and get outside your comfort zone. Dating is about taking risks. You simply can't have intimacy without vulnerability.

We trust you. We know that you're better off following your feelings than a bunch of arbitrary, outdated rules.

So trust yourself.

APPENDIX
DEBUNKING SOME
DATING RULES FOR MEN

JEFF

We almost didn't include this section, as we're guessing that the average reader of a book titled *It's Okay to Sleep with Him on the First Date* is not, in fact, a man. But the dumb dating rules affect both men and women alike, so here's a quick peek behind the curtain. Just a few of the rules that affect male behavior:

Wait two days to call her
The iconic rule from *Swingers*. I've seen the movie 793 times and consider it the greatest guy movie ever filmed, so please indulge me in a quick tangent. The irony is that people remember the rule from *Swingers*, but they forget that even here—where the rule originated—the rule is actually debunked.

Throughout the film Jon Favreau learns all these dating tips from Vince Vaughn, like "Don't be the guy in the PG movie. Be the guy in the R-rated movie." He learns to lie about the kind of car he drives. He exaggerates the success of his career. To meet women, he acts inauthentically. But once he meets Heather Graham? He just follows his instincts, acts naturally, and chucks the advice out the window. And it works.

The two-day rule *is* helpful, however, in helping him avoid rookie mistakes. The first time he gets a number, he calls her *that very night* and then bombs her with seven voice mails. So, like a lot of rules in this book, the two-day rule is a set of training wheels for people who don't really know any better...but it can be ignored with the right self-confidence.

This is something even the creators of the two-day rule acknowledge. On the ten-year anniversary DVD of the film, on a commentary track, Vaughn says that the two-day rule has gone away, and women want the guy to call right away to show that he's not a gamer.

Always pay on the first date

Yep. We agree with this rule (see pages 42–46).

Use a "neg"

Most women have probably been negged without even knowing it. Here's the theory, as mainstreamed by Neil Strauss's *The Game*, which reveals the secrets of pickup artists like "Mystery." If you say something negative to a woman, if you give her a backhanded compliment, like, "Wow, that haircut looks really expensive," you will make her feel insecure, which will, subconsciously, make her want to prove herself to you.

Just like with the "Men love bitches" rule (see pages 21–26), sure, there's something to the underlying psychology. It can work. But there's a difference between what *can* work and what *should* work. It's also true that a woman is more likely to sleep with a man if you roofie her; this doesn't mean you should do it. (That's a ridiculously unfair comparison, but the point is that *effective* doesn't mean *appropriate*.) It's bad karma. It's a type of dating trickery that has a way of coming back and haunting us. And if you're looking for a serious relationship, do you really want to meet your girlfriend/spouse by insulting her? And on a more pragmatic level, plenty of women have seen this tactic and can sniff it out.

Never show emotions

To some extent this is true. At the end of the day, do you really want to be a weepy, sentimental guy who cries whenever he sees a pretty dandelion? But adherence to this rule can be taken too far. Starting in Little League soccer, our culture encourages us to "man up" and never show emotions, which at times makes us seem distant and cold. Sometimes the problem isn't that we don't *feel* love; we just don't know how to show it.

Get her digits

In a recent book that delineates some "rules" for men, the author includes the rule "Know how to get digits." What this writer, Jeff Wilser, doesn't tell you is that plenty of men aren't Digit Guys. They have no aptitude for going into a bar, scanning the crowd, finding their "prey," and then chatting the girl up and scoring digits. Because they're not Digit Guys, they mistakenly think they're "not good at dating" and lose faith in the entire dating process. This is a shame. The meet-and-greet is only a small part of romantic relationships, and it's the least important part.

Good Digit Guys do not necessarily make good boyfriends, and vice versa.

Follow the three-second rule

Another gem from *The Game*. The thinking: you need to approach a woman in the first three seconds after you see her, or she'll think you're shy or a wimp. My friend (let's call him Dr. Cash) and I used to have a version of this: "He who hesitates is lost." And once again, just like many of the rules, there's a shred of truth behind the psychology—decisiveness *can* be attractive. But a slavish adherence to this rule can make you seem, act, and feel like a gamer. And if there's a woman you actually connect with, it doesn't really matter if you approach her in three seconds or three hours or three weeks or three years.

Impress her with your money/car/clothes

Ah, yes, the guy who makes a big show out of talking about his portfolio and casually mentions his yacht. Prick Alert 101.

Don't think of her as girlfriend material if she sleeps with you on the first date

Just making sure you're paying attention. This isn't a guy rule, and most guys don't really think this. Do some? Sure. There are still a few guys who will have a double-standard about sex on the first date, just like there are 15 percent of people who still approve of Congress.

ACKNOWLEDGMENTS

ANDREA

A few years ago Jeff and I met at a writing center in New York where there was a strict "no talking" policy (for two extroverts, this rule ain't easy). It wasn't long before we found ourselves gabbing in the communal eating area and discovered we had many similarities: we had both worked at NBC Universal Digital Studio at the same time (me as host of a show, Jeff as writer on a different show), we were both gearing up for the release of dating books (mine for women, Jeff's for men), and we both worked in finance* at the start of our careers.

We clicked immediately. Since then, Jeff and I have collaborated on many projects and have become good friends. Don't let

---

* That's not true. But I'm impressed that Jeff once worked in this field.

the fact that he looks like he could be in a boy band or a J.Crew ad distract you from who he really is—an incredibly thoughtful, smart, and really good guy with a big heart (though this line will make him cringe). Thank you, Jeff, for being there for me personally and professionally—for always taking the time to weigh in when I have questions and for offering your support. (I'll never forget when you held up my book poster in the 14th Street subway station to show it off to strangers!) I'm thrilled to have my name next to yours on this book.

Thank you to our literary agents, Ryan Harbage and Rob Weisbach, for all your amazing advice as we put this together. You pushed us to take a few more risks, and because of that, we believe in this project even more.

To our editor extraordinaire, Sarah Pelz, thank you for receiving our book with such enthusiasm and smarts. You helped us hone in on ideas, while maintaining our voice and vision. We had a feeling we were a "match" the first time we met you, and we were thrilled at the opportunity to work with you and your stellar team at Harlequin. (As a Canuck in the United States, I was also thrilled to work with a publisher that has its headquarters in my hometown of Toronto!) We also loved meeting Shara Alexander and thank her and Lathea Williams for working hard to promote *It's Okay to Sleep with Him.*

To my friends—there are way too many of you to mention by name—I continue to be so appreciative of your support throughout my book-writing process. (I generally transform into a hobbit when working on a manuscript.) I'm so lucky to have your support, in general. In particular, I'd like to thank two close friends, David Kaufman and Monika Rzezniczek McLaughlin, who provided valuable feedback in the editing stages of this book. From my perspective, either of them could be professional writers if they decided to switch careers.

This year has brought health scares and great challenges, and I'm more grateful than ever to my incredible family—Marilyn, Peter, and Veronica Syrtash. They always weigh in on my work with great insights and helpful edits. More important, though, they would drop (and have dropped) everything to be there for me...even when I didn't realize that I needed them. I love you and all that junk.

My in-laws, Ralph and Mimi Paoli, Tanya, Rob, Nola and Ness, David and Alex, and Jason Bell and his family—I'm so lucky to have you in my life. I'm also lucky that you still speak to me after I worked on a book about "surviving" your in-laws.

Finally, I've saved the best for last—my husband, Michael. Michael is too modest and has told me to save space in the acknowledgments to highlight others, so let me just say this: Thank you for always supporting me and for making me laugh every day.

JEFF

Thank you to every woman I've ever dated for not chopping off my head. Your clemency is more than I deserve.

Next, I need to thank a certain support group. For months I'd ask the same question of my close friends, colleagues, or dude I just met at the bagel stand: "Um, what do you think of the title *It's Okay to Sleep with Him on the First Date?*" It terrified me. I loved the overall philosophy—trust yourself, not the rules—but I feared that the money clause, "sleep with him," would be taken the wrong way and would Google haunt me to my grave. That's where my support group kicked in. This book would not have happened without you, my network of friends and bagel-stand compatriots, showing so much enthusiasm, letting me know that it's *empowering,* and encouraging me to do the project.

And no one was a bigger supporter than our amazing editor, Sarah Pelz, along with the entire team at Harlequin. Thanks, Sarah, for both nailing the big picture and diving into the trenches, and for allowing me to keep that mixed metaphor. A huge debt of gratitude to our agents, Rob Weisbach and Ryan Harbage. Rob, I know that this book tackles the rule about dating outside your league, but I still feel very, very lucky to have an agent so far out of my league. Thanks for everything you do.

Thanks to my family for not disowning me. Also to everyone who read early drafts of the manuscript, including Laura, Dan,

Cody (two-time reader! Cody, your ribbon's in the mail), Roxie, Katherine, Trevor, Kristine, Liz, Amy (your tough love really helped), Braxton, Captain Science, and Sarah. And thanks, Dave, for your detailed notes—much appreciated. Thanks, Keith, for the lifelong writing bromance. To Shawn, Lisa, Maya, and the Wednesday Night Writing Crew. And to all my friends who talked dating theories over the years: Adam, Terry, Steph, Paige, the other Steph, Jamie, Evan, Lee, Tara, Beth, Wes, Erik, Omer, Lisa, Teddy, Bizzle, Tania, Joe, Todd, Walker, Kate, James, and The Academy. Thanks, Xiao Li Tan and Krista, for the amazing last second photo shoot. Thank God we no longer use film, or else my Awkward Smile would have burned through thousands of dollars in expenses.

Thanks to Hakeem Olajuwon for 1994 and 1995. (Unrelated but still important.)

I think that's it. Oh, right. The most important person.

Here's the thing about Andrea. Not only is she the most charming, alluring, and dynamic person in the room, but she's also—somehow!—the best listener and the most empathetic. How is that even possible? Here's a typical afternoon with Andrea: We meet at a Brooklyn happy hour pub, she asks about my day, and I drone on and on about a wacky dating story, with her asking smart, probing questions, nodding, concentrating, deeply helping me with my silly problems. I'll talk more; she'll listen more. After two hours of this, I'll finally ask her, "What'd you do today?"

"Not much," she'll say. "I'm a little tired—sorry—because I had to get up at four a.m. to film a segment for the *Today* show. After that I did some counseling and saved a marriage. On the subway ride home there was an emergency, and I helped a woman deliver a baby. It was twins."

I was lucky as hell to meet Andrea. She pushes me to think harder and deeper, she actually provides analysis and substance, and she introduced me to a word called "research." I'm in awe of her command of relationship psychology, but I'm even more amazed that she can somehow, at the same time, sound so down-to-earth. There's a reason her clients and readers love her—whatever "it" is, she's got it. Her only flaw is questionable choices in male cowriters. Even more amazingly, smack in the middle of this project, she juggled some sobering Real Life Stuff with a coolness, grace, and sense of humor that puts the rest of us mere mortals to shame. Andrea, at the very least, I'm glad we've debunked the rule "Men and women can't be friends."

And finally, thank you to the girl from the 1994 Junior Statesmen of America Convention (see pages 137–140). If you're out there somewhere, call me. (Or text.)

INDEX

C

D

E

F

S

T

U

W

ABOUT THE AUTHORS

Andrea Syrtash is a relationship expert, author, and on-air personality. She has contributed to over a dozen relationship-advice books. She is the author of *He's Just Not Your Type (And That's a Good Thing)* and *Cheat On Your Husband (With Your Husband)* (Rodale Books).

Andrea regularly appears as a guest expert on shows, including the *Today* show, CBS *This Morning, The Wendy Williams Show,* VH1, and *On-Air with Ryan Seacrest;* and she has written for popular lifestyle sites, including OPRAH.com, Yahoo!, and MSN. She is the on-air host of *ON Dating,* produced by NBC Digital Studios; and co-host of *Life Story Project* on OWN: The Oprah Winfrey Network.

Jeff Wilser is a life coach. (Kidding. He's not even really sure what "life coach" means.) But he is a nationally syndicated relationship writer, and the author of *The Maxims of Manhood*, a collection of essays about being a guy. His writing has appeared in print or online in *Glamour, GQ, Esquire,* Today.com, VH1, *mental_floss,* and the *Los Angeles Times.*

He is the author of Pulitzer-bait *The Man Cave Book* (HarperCollins), and the founding editor of ThePlunge.com, the leading website for grooms. (Jeff has never been a groom.) Jeff is possibly the only person on the planet to have written for both *GQ* and *The Knot.* He can't tan.